SHORTER LIVES

By the same author

SHORTER LIVES

John A. Scott

PUNCHER & WATTMANN

First published in 2020

Published by Puncher and Wattmann
PO Box 279
Waratah NSW 2298

www.puncherandwattmann.com
puncherandwattmann@bigpond.com

NATIONAL
LIBRARY
OF AUSTRALIA

A catalogue entry for this book is available from the National Library of Australia.
ISBN   978-1-92578-048-2

Cover image
The Witnesses by Graeme Drendel
2008, oil on canvas, 137 x 183cm

Cover design & typesetting by Kate Francis
Printed by Lightning Source International

This project has been assisted by the Australian Government through the Australia Council, its arts funding and advisory body.

Australian Government

Australia
Council
for the Arts

In loving memory of

Margot Scott

*You should pretend to write about real people
and make it all up.*

Maynard Keynes, advice to Virginia Woolf,
25 May, 1921

RIMBAUD
A SHORTER LIFE

Charleville/Roche

It begins with leaving. In truth, several leavings. Delahaye catches one of the first, the poet's legs (long: like the scissor blades of the 'R' in his signature of 1870: best seen in the drawing *Nouveau Juif errant*) taking 'calm, formidable strides', his arms ('long' 'dangling') holding rhythm, eyes fixed to the distance. A 'resigned defiance', Delahaye puts it. 'Ready for anything', (away, beneath the shimmer of poplar leaves, their silver faces turning from an affront of wild air), '*sans* fear, *sans* anger,' writes Delahaye. 'Arriving from forever, the one who will go everywhere.' The returns, another matter entirely.

Here he is, emerging, late on this last-of-March afternoon from Mon. Jolly's café-flanked book-shop, where place Ducale meets rue du Moulin, in hand the latest *Parnasse Contemporaine* (blue covered, thirty-two uncut pages) comprising fifteen poems by Baudelaire: *Nouvelles Fleurs du Mal*, lent to him by Mon. Jolly in person with strict instructions it return in mint condition: that is, pages left uncut and without crease. Now back at the farmhouse in Roche, turning through the gatherings, noting five poems in their entirety; all of them intact, well-made and consequently of minor interest.

Elsewhere, mindful still of Jolly's instruction, R^{imb} edges the paper apart—*En parfait état*—the words return. No simple task with such vast hands; 'hands of a laundress', as Mallarmé will recall. 'Those of a strangler' as will Judge Théodore t'Serstevens, sentencer of Verlaine. He inclines the book to the lamp, peering inside the fissure of it, at the trembling spill of light, finds: *balconies of sky arisen from the waters' depth.* Re-shapes the hollow, tilting it lightwards, finds *a clochard sun passed-out beneath an arch.*

The following morning from two facing pages (the joined hands of them, as though in prayer), he scavenges words, half-lines. Evolves a syntax to bind them into phrases with no common sense. Misreads where necessary. In other words, takes liberties. Finds: *her body floating, gracious as the flimsy herds of snow!* These fragments disinterred by the fortuity of uncut pages from the mud of well-made lines. Asks: are not these the true poems of our times? Finds: *her charms pursuing all his vanished phantoms through the fogs of filth.*

He is pacing (coming, going) the room. The aim, he says to Delahaye, must be to eradicate not just the past (*les souvenirs*) but the future! Let us rid ourselves of hope (*l'espoir*), he spits, that most rancid of emotions. Let us embrace the absolute present. Now is the hour of exclamation! Now, the time of the unforeseen, and the totally forgotten! Now, the truest words are here! (*voici*) and there! (*voilà*), exploding in a frail imperiled present. *Cherchez l'inconnu!* he cries. *Trouvez Hortense!* Slapping the sweating flanks of the mattress.

***

R^{imb} writes to Paul Verlaine, author of *Poèmes Saturniens* with their tell-tale rhymes (of *hommes* and *sodomes*). *Is he the man of his poetry?* he asks of Bretagne, the go-between. Bretagne (even taking into account Verlaine's recent marriage to the sixteen-year old Mathilde Mauté, one of whose habits was using her feet to remove her hair ribbons) tells him *Yes, perhaps* too *much so. Dear great soul*, comes the reply. *We summon you. Await you.* Who arrives late September (with his large reddish hands; filthy-collared, necktie twisted. A clay pipe in his sulky and derisive mouth) holding to the rails—for what is drunkenness if not a journey?—of the newly-written 'Drunken Boat'.

Still undeniably a child. One, much younger than his not-yet seventeen years. One angered by his own inability to speak. Verlaine prepares to introduce his protégé to a gathering of the *Vilains Bonshommes. I don't know how to talk to them*, the intoxicated child admits. And here he is (blue hand-knitted socks prominent beneath his too-short trousers): blushing, overwhelmed in the company of these parlour-room poets—Mérat, Pelletan, Valade, d'Hervilly, Blémont, Creissels, Aicard. Here he is, forming fists to rub his eyes as might a four-year-old.

> You really missed out by not attending the latest dinner of the *Affreux Bonshommes*. There, under the auspices of Verlaine, his inventor, and myself, his John the Baptist on the Left Bank, was exhibited a terrifying poet of less than eighteen years called Arthur Rimbaud... this is the lad whose imagination, with its amazing powers and depravity, has been fascinating or frightening all our friends... Come and read his poems and judge for yourself. Unless this is one of Fate's nasty little tricks, we are witnessing the birth of a genius.
>
> Léon Valade

A Fizzy Drink
NOVEMBER, 1871

4.00 am in Place Pigalle's *Dead Rat* café, Charles Cros, early developer of the phonograph, the telegraph, theorist of colour photography; Charles Cros, chemist, *al*chemist, *poète* (he of the thick wavy hair draped upon his head like a sleeping badger) returns from the toilet to find his drink strangely animated. An hour earlier, R^{imb} is wiping his arse on vellum: pages torn from *L'Artiste*, a review which regularly features the poems of Charles Cros. On his way out, he slips a phial of sulphuric acid into his pocket and leaves without bothering to close the door.

Théâtre

Opening night on the boulevard.
A poet blowing smoke
in a cab-horse's nostrils.

***

R^{imb} appears a second time at the *Vilains Bonshommes*. On this occasion however, rather than show his poems, the *young genius* has chosen to read them aloud. And here he is, standing before them: a clumsy child-faced adolescent with a warbling, schoolboy's breaking voice; a yokel with an Ardennes accent strong as dialect. Thus delivered, the bizarre visions that had so beguiled them on the page, now strike them as ludicrous. They can barely contain their laughter.

Back in his seat, in the dark-timbered salon, he hatches disorder. Auguste Creissels stands to read his "Sonnet de combat" made from a 'straight, severe, properly laid out' double quatrain and a 'serious and rigid' tercet. At each line's end R^{imb} supplies an extra foot—(beat) *merde!* Carjat carries the 'little toad' from the room and throws him on the street. When the photographer leaves the meeting R^{imb} emerges from the darkness and stabs him in the stomach with Verlaine's cane-sword. That same night Carjat destroys the negatives of his two Rimbaud portraits.

R^{imb,} straight, severe, and properly laid out, surrenders to what he feels the *reasoned derangement* of sodomy. Embodying poetry as he does, R$^{imb's}$ very existence is an ultimatum: one requiring a choice between genius and taste. Verlaine turns against Mathilde (Miserable Carrot Fairy!) and their three-month-old son, Georges, as though they alone have kept him from heaven. Each night he returns, crazed on absinthe or hashish. He beats his wife. Half-strangles her. Tries to set her hair aflame. He throws his child against the wall. The sulking boy has driven him insane.

***

Fleeing the chaos, Rimb returns to Roche where he begins work on Un Saison en Enfer. Verlaine writes to his lover, who cuts the letter open in the toilet, using the crude clasp knife he now affects. My God, he reads, you have wounded me, wounded me with love, and the wound is quivering still. Rimb is not overly fond of wounding his elder's quivering hole. Généralement, it is Verlaine who does the wounding. And, it would seem, for most of the night. 'It was impossible to keep my shit inside,' Rimb (recently returned to Paris) complains to anyone prepared to listen.

***

Vowels

A, the oddly tapering glans;
Ɛ, the epsilon of buttocks
(with their papules and pustules);
I, the swollen purplish shaft;
U, the hanging scrotal sack;
O, the trou du cul itself.

***

The older man gazes down upon the sulking R^{imb's} arsehole (which also seems to sulk) dark and wrinkled like a carnation†. Dreaming of those *nuits d'exception*, when the boy acquiesces to his request, when he (suffering an adorable malignancy of fever) feels himself engulfed by the *gamin's* vast soiled plumage: when, chosen, damned, surrounded by an immense unknown breath, the hard angel pummels him—sweet delirium, blessed fear—between the shoulders. He crawls forward, (Now!) he is there, here is all of him! *Mount my back*, he cries, *trample!*

---

†In some versions, 'like a pink' (of genus *Dianthus*). Other versions, citing a hydrangea, a tulip, a Savoy cabbage and a black ear fungus, seem unlikely and probably reflect the respective translators' own fantasies.

***

Two Rooms

1

There is not much
space here with all the boxes
and bins   though at any moment
the room opens to a turquoise
blue sky   The outer walls are
overgrown with birthwort
where the imps vibrate
their gums   He spends the nights
drinking water against
the summer heat   so thirsty
he grows scared of gangrene
    Discontented godmothers
clamber into the sideboards
and remain there.

2

He works at night now. From midnight to five in the morning. His room looks out over a garden of the Lycée Saint-Louis. There are enormous trees beneath his narrow window. At three in the morning, the candle fades: all the birds cry at once in the trees: it's over. No more work. He has to look at the trees, the skies, gripped by that inexpressible hour, the first in the morning. He sees the lycée dormitories, absolutely mute. And already the noise of the tip carts in the boulevards: disjointed, sonorous, delicious. At five o'clock he goes down to buy bread—it is time. Workers are walking everywhere. It is time for him to visit the local wine merchants and get drunk.

***

R^{imb} & Verlaine depart for London where they find accommodation in an upstairs room at N^{o.}8, Great College Street, Camden Town. R^{imb} works on his *Illuminations*—Verlaine's presence an increasingly unwanted distraction. He grows disgusted by the clumps of Verlaine's hair which appear across the pillows, in the drain of the sink. The older poet makes attempts to hide them, in the backs of drawers, in a cupboard's dark corners: a drunkard's piteous attempts to hide the empty bottles of *absinthe*. He has become impossible to live with: he is bone idle, he is rarely sober, and is *misbehaving with people of their acquaintance*.

'People are saying I'm a pederast,' he sobs, 'but I'm not! I'm not!'

Mathilde, abandoned in Paris, prepares for divorce. Verlaine writes to his long-standing friend Edmond Lepelletier asking him to oversee the publication of his *Romances sans paroles*—I am going to kill myself, he says.

***

Sidling from its display in the gunsmith's shop in galeries Saint-Hubert (thereby fulfilling Max Jacob's maxim), *the revolver seeks its natural owner.* It is Verlaine who finds a Le Faucheux 7mm six-shot sitting comfortably within his palm; on the counter, within easy reach, is a box of fifty cartridges. Later, in a rue des Chartreux bar, following his memory of the gunsmith's instructions, he loads three of the fifty— why only *three*, you wonder, quite rightfully—into the gun, and orders yet another drink. Everything tumbles towards that overly-reported (yet no less frightful) business.

After the deluge of argument, Verlaine fires two of the three bullets he has loaded in the revolver: one of which hits the hotel room's wall, the other, more famously, his lover's wrist. For R^{imb}, the situation is out of control. He will leave for Paris, thence to Charleville and Roche, that night. At the Gare de Midi, Verlaine, in pursuit of his lover, reappears—he will use the gun again, he says (against R^{imb}, against himself?) Terrified, the young anarchist runs to the arms of the conveniently passing-by Constable Auguste Michel who places the older poet under arrest.

The following morning Verlaine's genitalia are the subject of detailed observation, not by another poet seeking inspiration for a sonnet, but by doctors Vleminckx & Semal. They find his uncut penis to be *short and unvoluminous, the glans, in particular, small and tapering. By a slight parting of the buttocks*, they instruct, *the anus can be dilated to a depth of about one inch. This movement reveals a widened infundibulum, resembling a truncated cone with a concave apex.* Concluding thus, that: *Verlaine bears on his person traces of habitual pederasty, both active and passive. Neither type of trace is sufficiently marked to give grounds for suspecting inveterate and long-standing habits; rather, they would indicate fairly recent practices...*

***

All of which, now raised, is best not dwelt upon. The sulking poet, so desirous of extremity, hastens home in terror of the same. R^{imb,} back in Roche, completes his *Un Saison en Enfer*, thereby conferring legend on his life; making for himself a perfect avatar: *poète monstrueuse et invisible.* In Paris, Verlaine is fined 200F and sentenced to 2yrs hard labour. R^{imb} collects his author's copies of *Saison* from Mon. Jacques Poot and C°, 37 rue aux Choux, Brussels, distributing seven copies to his friends and acquaintances and feeds the remainder one-by-one into the flames of the family hearth.

Caught in this act, he catches, from behind, his thirteen-year-old sister, Isabelle, angled in the doorway. *What are you doing?* she asks. Burning my books. Art is an idiocy. This book *in particular* (and he waves a copy above his head) is living proof of literature's absurdity.

Verlaine writes to Victor Hugo asking him to intervene in his unfortunate circumstances. The Great French Poet and Novelist suggests he 'show patience'.

A Future for Rimbaud

How might we consider Rimbaud had Verlaine emptied a *fully-loaded* gun into the young poet's body: wrist, chest, stomach, thigh, groin, heart, adding to the pair of Carjat portraits (their negatives long since destroyed and taken away by a tip cart, one early morning— disjointed, sonorous, delicious) of October puffy-faced and December thin-lipped, necktie askew of 1871, a third image, courtesy of the gendarmerie, showing the poet's face frozen in an agony: the 'child' still visible, though, disappointingly, with no trace of the sulkiness. What now would be made of the *gamin*, dead at eighteen, on the floor of a hotel room, with *Season in Hell* unfinished; and only a handful of *Illuminations*?

Or what if Rimbaud, back at Roche, thankful to be alive, found himself shocked free of poetry: taking up, in its stead, musical composition? Delahaye relates in his *Delahaye témoin de Rimbaud* how his friend had for some time aspired to be a pianist. Indeed, so strong was this desire that he had carved a practice keyboard into the table of his upstairs room. The young church organist, Louis Létrange, from whom Rimbaud had sought lessons in the rudiments of music, noted that he was seeking 'new sonorities'. Delahaye goes on to say that Rimbaud (frustrated by the lack of a loud pedal or the lack of sound in general?), took it upon himself to order a piano, which he had hoisted to his upstairs bedroom at the farmhouse. What is more, courtesy of

Verlaine we have a sketch showing the young unruly-haired poet perched at an upright piano, playing with an almost Lisztian fervour:

Happily, these speculations need not concern us. Both *Un Saison en Enfer* and *Illuminations* were completed and, with them, Rimbaud's place in world literature was assured. Not content however with producing two indisputable masterpieces, he had created *une vie de bohème* to accompany them; a suite of scandalous actions such as would be preserved in any number of diaries, notebooks and memoirs. He had made a monster to equal Frankenstein's and, even more astonishing, fashioned it from himself. All that remained to be achieved was the creation of the total *absence* of it all.

Villes
[LONDON]

Stench of musk and coal-smoke. A sun rolls in its permanent eclipse through a receding, descending sky; whilst bridge upon bridge, encumbered with hovels, arch in sympathy. On the dome-laden riversides, cathedrals, parliaments and mausoleums dwindle and sink. R^{imb,} recently returned to London, has rented the basement of 178 STAMFORD STREET, backing onto the treacherous grey-blue *manche* which is the Thames. No rue Monsieur-le-Prince with its views of enormous trees and the empty dormitories of the Lycée Saint-Louis.

Here, the view is given by a narrow, horizontal window, level with the footpath outside, and gained only by standing on a chair. Here comes a widow's charcoal dress; here a flurrying dachshund with eight countable tails. Now come a flock of trouser cuffs; the clack of a dozen walking canes. Now, the jet-black perambulators. A Tidal Chart (included as part of the rent) means water levels for the room are predictable and easily enough accommodated. Deeper, are the drains of which nothing permits itself to be described.

Cross-legged on the table top, with the Thames an ugly thrashing water below, R^{imb} (despite the book-burning at Roche) is working on *Villes*—a new *Illumination*. In the hours of the waters' full retreat, he descends: taking up the refashioning of his wardrobe and bedstead. A fortnight later, he sails off in his green-painted *bâteau-armoire-lit* (pulling to the river mouth with its fermenting swamps, amongst whose reeds lie vast wicker creels, in one of which rots an entire leviathan) making for Alexandria.

✳✳✳

Villes
[ADEN]

This is not Alexandria.

Here, there isn't a single tree, even a desiccated one, nor blade of grass, nor fertile ground, nor a drop of fresh water. The city is an extinct volcanic crater filled to the brim with sand from the sea. One sees and touches nothing but lava and sand. What is worse: the crater's walls prohibit any air from entering the city in which one roasts as if inside a lime kiln.

Around the crater's rim are *colossi* with likenesses of the great men of literature. They offer up mouldering books whose pages have been eaten by years of sulphuric rain. Once, from the footbridges over the abyss, scholars trumpeted these men's achievement. Now, they are discredited—objects of derision. They have met here to observe the last of you, a living frame for one more picture!

At some distance from the city is a doorless tower made from the finest of ivories. There is a single window, high in the walls, from which flows an appalling black smoke. Even the most erudite and loquacious who approach the tower lose the ability to speak. Their silence quickly filling with the sound of a relentless mastication of hair.

Villes
[HÀRAR]

The streets of Hàrar are largely steep and narrow spaces, riddled with rock, which meander between a mix of mud and stone terraces, and conical huts. When rain arrives from the surrounding hills these streets are re-born as veering rivers. Then there are the stenches, with their odious blendings of rot, of livestock slaughtered mid-street, and the sickly rose-tinge of leprosy. Dawn in the city brings donkey-bray and the falsetto chant and bicker of the Hàrari women as they move between the houses and their garden wells. Slender, smooth-skinned women; golden-faced. With nightfall comes the howl and the treacherous, stupid, laughter of hyenas. In the House of Raouf Pasha, where Rimbaud is accommodated, one can watch lines of flat grey ants swarm across the roof beams.

***

This will be his new home, new life. He will work for Viannay, Bardey & Co., traders in coffee, ivory, hides, incense, musk.... Later in his time he will consolidate his commercial activity into gun-running—outmoded/ outdated rifles (in France worth seven francs a piece.)

He is now known by a new name: ABDO RINBO. His new appearance is known from the handful of photographs—in particular the self-portrait 'with arms folded'. White suit. Its buttonless top to all intents an unlaced straitjacket. His fez set well back on his head. Rimbaud, the sulking poet, was last seen somewhere in Herer, Hazar, Horor...

In Hàrar, it is a February afternoon and the French trader surrenders to the graceful beauty of one (or another), of the nameless straight shouldered, narrow hipped, high-breasted Adari women.

With April, Jacaranda flowers cover the streets, battered from the branches by a deluge of hailstones.

The gutters are flushed by rust-coloured storm-water. April, and Rinbo is unwell. Bardey joins his employee and notes 'the unmistakable marks of syphilis in his mouth'.

***

Donna Abissina

Rinbo takes a Christian Abyssinian girl as a companion. He has either purchased her in Hàrar, or somewhere in 'the desert' from Oblock on the Red Sea; unless at a slave market in nearby Tadjourah. Françoise Grisard, who comes every Sunday afternoon to Rinbo's house to do cleaning, describes her as tall and slender, *assez jolie*; her skin coffee-coloured rather than black, and dressed in European style. She smokes cigarettes. Her relationship with Rinbo, Françoise assures us, was intimate. Ottorino Rosa, an Italian trader, photographs this 'Donna Abissina', her body white-shawled; her hair white-scarved. In October, 1885, Rinbo sends her back to Abyssinia.

***

An omen of the end arrives—for the end itself has not yet begun—the *Matin de Deux Mille Chiens*. The morning of two thousand dogs.

ABDO RINBO lives nearby the meat market, where dogs of this town quarter regularly feast on offal. Recently however, they have taken to pissing on his coffee bales. Pissing on the hides hung outside on the terrace of his house to dry.

One evening, tired of the dogs' incessant marking, he distributes a wide semi-circle of strychnine pellets in the dust of the street before his house.

With first light of day he is woken by cries of outrage. He makes his way to the porch. Before him lie a vast swathe of dead and dying animals: hyenas, vultures, bustards, eagles, ostriches. A flock of scarlet pigeons. Much of a flock of sheep. Large-headed black boars, monkeys (large-maned and dog-snouted), giant mole rats. Simien jackals. A green-backed turtle; a white-eyed gull. And ranged about them all, dogs. Two thousand, as reckoned by one priest.

He is given a new name: *Rinbo, terror of dogs*. He will be badly beaten several times in coming weeks. He will narrowly escape lynching.

The end itself begins with sledgehammer blows to the right knee, only, it seems, struck as if from *beneath* the flesh. It begins with a leg that swells thicker below the knee than above.

He writes to his mother: 'send a stocking, the best, a long silk stocking'.

Now, the pain is more like a nail battered through the knee, side-on. *Now*, the whole leg stiffens as if made from one solid, jointless, bone; the kneecap swollen to a *boule* likeness, immobile, 'drowning in secretions' (ineffable pain).

Voyage

1

Another end begins with the reddish mass of Hàrar shrinking at the horizon, as if it were the *town* which was leaving: a magical illusion he will never see again. He has determined to make passage back to Aden. And from Aden to Marseilles; a funeral procession acted out before the death. He has had a litter made—two long carrying poles with a low wooden frame lashed onto them, and a canvas cover. One of the four litter-bearers is blighted by vitiligo—marked piebald for life. He will act as a map.

2

He travels beneath the hemisphere of a god's eye; whose blinks—lid closing over—appear to him as hours of darkness falling instantly across the sky. On this final passage to Aden, pain serves to remind him of the unbearable present—that gasp between the insufferable past and an intolerable future. It is the first day, and the litter breaks apart. He has never felt the weight of such misery. No solace to be found, no pity to be had, from those about him—perhaps each of them with miseries the equal of his own.

3

The most recurrent of the Baudelaire fragments that come back to him is from *Le Gouffre*. Pit. Abyss. Not in the form of a memory, but materialising everywhere about him.

> *The fear   I feel*
>   *suddenly*
> *overtaking the wind*
>
> *everywhere, to the depths*
>   *the strand (sea shore, beach)*
> *terrifying, captivating*
>
> *My God-nights, of His knowing hand*
>   *nightmare,*
>   *multitudinous,*
>   *unrelenting*
>
> *sleep*
> *like the fear of a great pit*
> *carries him away*
>
> *empty*
> *vacant*
>
> *a horror leading who knows where*
> *infinity through every window—*
> *haunted*
> *vertiginous*

4

He has been obliged to travel in the Season of Storms and on the fourth day (far ahead of the caravan), he is caught in open country. It rains for sixteen hours without cease. He lies on the litter, on his back, uncovered. His eyes are battered beneath closed eyelids. He calls for a cloth to be laid across his face. The material becomes soaked almost before it is fully laid. He can only breathe mouthfuls of drenched cottons. The cloth is drowning him. He flails with exhausted arms. Clutches at a corner. Drags the tenacious material from his face. Once more it begins: the rain-pelt at his lids. As if it would crush the ingredients of his eyes to pulp in the mortar of his sockets.

5

The camels suffer terrible bloating. Their bellies distended almost to the ground. Humps appearing in their flanks. And his knee as if somehow it had become infected by the same disease. The bearers march badly. Continuously out of step. When they arrive at Arrouina they throw him down on the ground. He fines them a thaler each.

The journal is abandoned. He has lost patience with its subject. Besides, re-living the journey once more in its description becomes unbearable. He is worn out and paralysed by the movement of the lying still. A wingless butterfly.

The entourage arrives at Zeilah wharf, from where they will board a boat to Aden. And three days at sea without food.

***

He is unloaded at the docks—*winched* over the salt-washed boards. The sudden bird's eye view brings back another fragment from the pillaged Baudelaire. The laments of an Icarus. He, as much as his predecessor, seeking both the end and the centre of space, arms racked by such unaccustomed beating. His eyes burn out long before the softening of the wax; he falls, possessing only memories of the sun. Of darkness where the sun should be. He sits on the quay, amongst the packing cases, each of them an unknown city— Huràr, Huzar, Horor.

His world quickly narrows to a room at the European Hospital in Aden. There is an English doctor, he fails to catch his name: Nokes? Nouks? Naulks? One of them. Many things have become uncertain. Nokes (or...) diagnoses synovitis—a disease of the liquids of the knee. The cap, he says, must be removed.

Mid-way through the operation R^{imb} briefly wakes to see the shallow dish of his kneecap being placed in a shallow dish. From where he lies, prone on the operating table, he can make out that its surface has been decorated with elaborate scrimshaw.

His only thought now is a return to France 'I am

scared' he dares write in his letters; and it is a fear far greater than that he had felt at the railway station in Brussels staring at the revolver in Verlaine's hand. His leg is now enormous; to use his own words, like 'a giant pumpkin'. He will be left a cripple. He leaves immediately for Marseilles on the passenger ship, *L'Amazone*.

***

From his room, a glimpse of the colonnaded courtyard. *L'hôpital de la Conception*. R[imb's] right leg has been amputated; the stump disgustingly short. He is very sick, very sick. Life has become impossible for him. How wretched he now is... Mère Rimbaud—the Mouth of Darkness—has come from Roche to his bedside. She quickly tires of his endlessly reiterated miseries.

My hands cannot hold anything. When I am walking I cannot look at anything but my solitary foot and the ends of the crutches. Your head and shoulders slope forward, and you slump along like a hunchback. You tremble at the sight of objects and people moving around you, frightened they're going to knock you over and break the other leg. People sneer at the way you hop along. When you sit back down you have lifeless hands, and armpits rubbed raw, and the face of an idiot...

'Never let yourself be amputated,' he is telling *la Bouche d'Ombre*. 'Better to suffer a year in hell than to be amputated.' He leans across and takes a drink from his right kneecap which he now uses for drinking water. 'Let them butcher you,' he continues, 'flay you, slice you to pieces, but never allow anyone to amputate you.' Mère Rimbaud tells him she has no intention of being amputated. Within two weeks she is gone. He will never speak, never write, to her again, this one-legged man with his grey hair, his dark skin and his 'furious eye'.

***

R[imb's] younger sister, Isabelle, takes her mother's place. Upright, oval-faced, eyebrows joined, slight double-chin, droopy-eyed, small turned-up nose and pursed-lipped: a spinster, uncomfortable in her 'best clothes', dowdy, plain, and lacking in confidence... *Provincial*.

Never let yourself be amputated,' he is telling her. 'Better to suffer a year in hell than to be amputated. Let them butcher you, flay you, slice you to pieces, but never allow anyone to amputate you.'

R^{imb} decides to return to Roche.

✳✳✳

In the Ardennes, a sudden early Autumn. He has stayed at the farm a month in his upstairs room (at his own request), he, who cannot climb or descend stairs, huddled with his few possessions: books on science and geography; assorted lengths of Ethiopian cloth; a wax seal: ABDO RINBO; and an Abyssinian harp.

Obedient to its abrupt and unexpected command, *millefeuille* (this glorious confection of a thousand-leaves), the poplars, once again, have turned their shimmering silver faces from the wind.

The neighbours complain amongst themselves as to what is worse: the constant moaning; the raving, the cursing, often until dawn; or the childish refrains coming from the small self-playing reed organ ill-advisedly installed by his mother to 'comfort' him.

When he dreams, it is of his sick-bed in Marseilles. At the door, a packing case has been delivered. He staggers from the bed. He splinters back the boards (ones he would once have saved for shelving), ravenous to learn the contents of this special delivery. Inside, he finds a consignment of Verlaine's pistols; a consignment of wounded wrists.[†] For Isabelle it is only towards the end of her brother's stay that she learns he was once a poet. From this she understands the obligation to write a biography. There are many memories to be recorded for posterity. Let alone a detailed chronicle of his final days. She begins taking notes.

[†] The image of wounded wrists (as if by shackles) has been cited as a possible source of the myth of Rimbaud's participation in the slave trade.

✳✳✳

Accompanied by Isabelle, R^{imb} returns to Marseilles, a natural embarkation point for Africa. By now he has lost the use of his right arm—it hangs at his side, the desiccated outcrop of a shrivelled body. A specially ordered wooden leg arrives in a box reminiscent of a coffin. He will never adopt it. Wracking, as it does, his body with every step.

The doctors say his condition is a transmission, through the bone marrow, of the cancer which necessitated the amputation. The doctors say he will not recover.

Baudelaire's 'Malabaraise' haunts him, often in the guise of his Abyssinian mistress (that *assez jolie* woman in her Western clothes). In the very first of pre-dawn light, he discerns her moving about his room, filling the water jug, chasing out a persistent fly. He sees her through the flimsy snow that falls softly to the blanket and the floor. 'My wife,' he calls, yet no sound issues from his mouth. 'My wife,' he calls again. But already she has gone, back to Abyssinia, pursuing other vanished phantoms *through the fogs of filth.*

Late one night, Isabelle awakens to a strange music from her brother's room. She enters to find him propped against a wall upon a high cushion. His left leg is crossed over the remnant of the thigh of his right, but there seems not the slightest lack of ease in his posture. As though in a trance, he is playing the Abyssinian harp he had brought with him from Hàrar. Isabelle, moved by what she has witnessed, brings from her travel case pencil and paper and renders a sketch of this transcendent moment.[†]

[†] It has been demonstrated that the 'Abyssinian harp episode' was a colourful invention of Isabelle's, added to her 'memories' of Rimbaud in his final days. It appears that in 1911, twenty years after her brother's death, Isabelle came across a drawing of an Abyssinian harpist in a magazine. She made a tracing of the illustration and sketched-in her brother's head. See S. Murphy. '"J'ai tous les talents!": Rimbaud harpiste et dessinateur'. *Parade Sauvage. Bulletin*, 6. (November, 1990, pp. 28–49.)

***

His sentences, soft, slow, now contain words from many languages—both European and Oriental. Words throated and smooth-tongued, doggish barkings and proclamations worthy of kings. He lies in his bed with its rounded metal-headboard and its thin, grey, blanket.

Outside, furious rainstorms. A sky swirled out by the mad one-eared Dutch Impressionist or, yes, Soutine (who is as yet unborn).

He calls Isabelle close, tells her how during the night the nurses and the nuns come into his room and do abominable things to him.

Are you certain?

There is no doubt about it.

A large growth has appeared between his hip and his stomach.

***

Baudelaire, now a distant voice, drifts to him, late, in fragments from the uncut book. He finds these words from the blue-covered volume make perfect sense.

Beyond, sing like
the wind   a keening from who
knows where   the ear and however
'Yes, gentle voice, that one
is able, alas, to name
behind the scenes and often, facts
I fall into   console   say 'Keep
not as beautiful as...'

waves of slow languor
fed by an invisible slope
flowed into the depth of my heart
Insensibility
from numbers
and beings.

Lot 1 single tusk only
Lot 2 two tusks
Lot 3 three tusks
Lot 4 four tusks
Lot 5 two tusks

A Future for Rimbaud

Arthur Rimbaud misses seeing the Twentieth Century by nine years and three weeks. How different if he had chosen to resist the desire to lie with one of the beautiful Adari women. There would have been no syphilis with its ultimate life-taking consequences. Not long after his death (which we shall now agree failed to happen on November 10th 1891) circumstances would soon dramatically change for the people of Hàrar. Between 1888 and 1892 Rinderpest introduced from India killed approximately 90% of cattle in Abyssinia. Lack of rainfall from November 1888 led to famine in all but southernmost provinces; locusts and caterpillar infestations destroyed crops in Akele Guzay, Begemder, Shewa and around Hàrar. Conditions worsened with cholera outbreaks, a typhus epidemic, and a major smallpox epidemic. Conditions even obliged the coronation of Menelik II to be a subdued event. The First Italo-Ethiopian War was only five years away.

But that is neither here nor there. Rimbaud is still alive and in reasonable health. He makes his way back to Europe. His years of vigorous walking over mountain ranges having taken their toll on his legs, he now affects a sedan chair carried by two faithful Abyssinian natives he has met in a Paris bar. His skull in his later middle age has taken on the precise dimensions of his fez (as seems predicted in the 1875 drawing *La tronche Machin* by Ernest Delahaye) allowing him to stain his shaved skull with red pigment, thereby acquiring a permanent headpiece. It delivers to him a startling anonymity. In 1911-12 his travels lead him, restlessly still, to Venice (to which city he unknowingly carries Abyssinian Cholera, a virulent strain which causes the death of both Mann's and Visconti's Aschenbachs), where he can be sometimes glimpsed travelling on the Grand Canal, his chair high in a low barge, *l'uno con una gamba sola. L'eccentrico*, who, it is said, once wrote an equally eccentric poetry. He returns in the early evenings to the Grand Hôtel des Bains, Lungomare Marconi 41, on the East Shore of the Lido. He sits at the piano. He has carved a keyboard into its closed lid and plays, *tutti, ma in silenzio*.

At the outbreak of WWI, he is close to sixty years old. He briefly becomes a war correspondent for *Le Monde*, finding the sedan chair a great impediment on the battlefields, but long enough to see his native country's northern plain as nothing if not another desert—one of wetness to the Abyssinian dryness—a treeless swathe of mud, mixed through with flesh.

With peace restored to Europe he finds time to turn through the pages of the latest literary journals. He reads new poetries—Futurist, Vorticist, Dadaist, and detects no small influence of his own *oeuvre*. He reads how Charles Cros (now affecting a real badger upon his head) has founded a new art movement by the name of Surrealism. Most surprising, but gratifyingly so, he finds his own poetry to be everywhere exalted, by generation after generation. Perhaps he grows fond of poetry again. Perhaps he even considers writing some new *Illuminations*?

In his seventies, he seeks out his old friend, the recently deceased writer, Ernest Delahaye, who, after a successful career as a civil servant at the Education Ministry, has written *mémoires* of both Rimbaud and Verlaine. With Rimbaud's reappearance in Roche, Delahaye acknowledges the immediate necessity for a further chapter to his biography. But Rimbaud stays his hand. After some discussions, the two men come to an agreement, finding it better—more poetic—to leave the poet dead in the *Hôpital de la Conception*, Marseilles, with the angels of flame and ice.

CHARLES CROS
SIX SONNETS

From October 17th to November 15th, 1871, Arthur Rimbaud, not long arrived in Paris, found lodgings in the laboratory-studio of the chemist, photographer and independent inventor of the phonograph, Charles Cros. With Rimbaud's departure, Cros, also a poet of interest in Paris of the era, came to fully embrace the young boy's advocacy of a 'rational disordering of all the senses' and liberated his previously well-made sonnets. This project began with an untitled sonnet-sequence composed in English.

● Indicates ink blot in original

Wanderer

In the bewildered and aimless
race of my life I cross bitter mountains
and insidious valleys—the *Vale of Laughter;*
Vale of Rats—with the pride of adventurous
Englishwomen. My trail, I know, will not be
quickly followed. On the high peaks that no
prudence would envy, what purpose clocks,
●igs, mirrors, fields of herring? The music
of a crystal night resonates in my head the
rhythm of the coming day. I rise to the peals
of departure. My heart, once *langsam*, thrills
within the serenity of the planetary radius.
A fresh wind swells my accordion. I draw
breath from being long awaited everywhere.

Revolt

By dint of being blond, her hair
breaks in waves on my pillow, crimped
by confused accents which turn *vous êtes*
into summer. Absurder still, since we no
longer speak in English, other than in
clouded keepsakes. I still have memories
rendered in an old enamel which portrays
a naive and a gentle people only rarely kissed.
It has haunted me since green wood took a
tone of emerald impossible to find within
the Salon; in the same way her skin is
sometimes the reason I lose all respect for
whiteness that the Classical admits: lilies,
    snow etc. How it infuriates me!

Roistering (I)

Through the heavy nights
and questionable mornings you live
in garish cafes, haunted by whores,
knowing how you will rush to Mass
on account of your dissolving fibres.
Already there are poets swarming on
Tour Eiffel, tired of glamour, yet thrilled
by the wild lawns of Summer's end:
these sudden panoramas impaled by
the approach of a reality which, even
in semblance, they have seen enough of,
like those eyes with their gushing violet
rays, awoken by ominous lightning
    one warm cloudless night.

Roistering (II)

You awake in the gutters
of Les Halles, blushing at the sight
of fishmongers whose overalls un-
leash the smell of eager mackerels.
Gardeners, ignorant of such humours
gather cabbages from the pavement.
The touter from a nearby brothel wears
a spiral hat of Chinese silk to counter-
point his *roufflaquette* (or 'lovelock',
if you have English, but little French).
Would you like her hair a deeper mauve?
he asks. *Or shorn completely? Might I
recommend a* Muscadet *to complement
a lover's sudden b●ldness.*

Sonnet: To Mlle de S. L. C.

The adolescent herring
has a hard, proud flesh, and bright
green eyes reminiscent of la *Limousin*
liqueur. For me, it brings back those
nights in Chaudy—the sound of hurdy-
gurdys and *chàbrettes* (or 'bagpipes',
if you have English, but little French).
My dear Mademoiselle de S. L. C.
having *longtemps* sampled lilies, snow,
I think increasingly of muscular and
hirsute lovers with fleet fish-flavoured
hair—like you—their eyes, gushing violet
rays, revealing a supreme truth, sans
ice, absolute, ineffable.

Sonnet: To Mme N.

Chère Madame with your skin as
narcotic as it is nacreous (top-capped and
with culvert ribbon in your hair), living
youth pours from you, for whom absinthe
and Paleophones are equally *passé*. Our
lives shall have the smoothness of red
herrings mating on a bed of ●ats. Madame,
by my teeth, let me transcend descriptions
of your eyes as placid silver lakes. Salt-bitten,
smoke-gnawed, we shall make immoral
love in an unlocked hotel room or (better
still), a slow-moving *fiacre* lacking blinds,
whilst I declaim my sonnets which out-
    shine the frying of eels.

VIRGINIA STEPHEN
PART ONE OF
A SHORTER LIFE

for Michael Cunningham

To their marriage in 1878, Julia Duckworth brought three children (George, Stella & Gerald); Leslie Stephen, the one (Laura). Over the next four years an equal number of offspring were born into this new union—Vanessa, Thoby, Adeline Virginia & Adrian. The steadily growing household was, with increasing difficulty, accommodated at the Duckworth's terrace in a Kensington cul-de-sac: N° 22 Hyde Park Gate. In 1881, whilst on a walking tour in Cornwall, Leslie Stephen saw and immediately purchased the lease on a mid-nineteenth Century house (newly restored after the fire of 1873), in the town of St. Ives. From that point onwards it became the habit of the Stephen family to spend their summer holidays at *Talland House.*

Talland House

The Cornish Express
carries them from Paddington to St Erth,
(it is the summer of 1888,
a year endlessly recited by the wheels
along their tracks) where they take the branch line
to St Ives. From there the Stephen household
makes its various paths up the hill to *Talland.*
Lagging behind, the servants struggle under
ill-fitting luggages—various arrange-
ments of *portmanteaux*, trunks, and cases—pre-
cursors every one of them (Vanessa glances
back in their direction) of a cubist
revolution still some years away. These
    are the long summers,

stretching August to
October. The 'Times of Childhood'. Here, at
Talland, and its *Gardens*. Three sloping acres,
amongst which sit levelled, hedged, spaces each
with its family name and history—Kitchen
Garden, Coffee Garden (with *the profusions
of escallonia*); the orchard, straw-
berry beds, glasshouses and the Cricket Ground.
Stella writes of the heat of these mid-August
days, of Cricket after tea; of playing late
into the evening with a luminous ball.
She mentions a day of *'Wild Cricket'* (without
details). And takes a photograph of Ginny
    (bowler), Nessa (batsman),

    hair tied back from their
faces. Dressed identically in the dark
cloth of their sisterhood. Such sights will be
with her forever. The house, yes—its flat-roof
edged by criss-cross railing. The tall French bay
windows. The walls with their statueless arches
each awaiting an eminent Victorian.
But most, *the Gardens*. The light which passes
through them, from noon-glare to the shading-down.
The rampage of `profuse, disorderly`
`flower-beds` before the windows—descriptions
endlessly transcribed by biographers.
`The passion flower reaching upwards to`
    `the balcony` where

    her mother—Julia—
appears (white gowned) to bless her life. Below,
beyond the house, St Ives, as she imagines
(quite impossibly so) it must always
have been, this fishing town; and she about
the writing of it, once more, her memory
of it—`steep, windy, noisy`—`narrow-streeted`
town, with `no arrangement`. A many curved
bay, edged with slips of sand and greened sand hills
behind. The blue vein of the R^{iv} Hayle
across the sand, with marking stakes along
its channel into the Harbour. A basin
of water she finds forever changing
    colour; now deep blue;

now emerald green;
at once a purple and white-crested stormy grey.
In this `windy, noisy, fishy` town her
mother ministers to the poor, the sick.
She, once the model for the Virgin Mary
(and she pregnant with Vanessa)—Burne-Jones'
Annunciation. 'Epiphany' of
the angelic vastness hovering, weightless
and all weight, before her mother—Julia—
beautiful mother, cloaked, hair bundled beneath
a mushroom hat. The child-Virginia, *Ginny*,
waits for her on the beach; the waves breaking
gently in their two-fold motion. She chooses
    beach pebbles by ancient

    means—palm-feel, colour-depth,
else startlingly pied, and by their sound as they
are brought against each other. She pockets them.
Each day a similar number—no less
than three. No more than five. Raises her head
to the wave break. Scores it in her mind, *one-two,*
one-two, unknowingly immortalising
its rhythm. With, beyond, the vast sleeve of
the English Channel encircling Godrevy
Island. With its *lighthouse.* And she, lying half-
awake, in bed, at *Talland*, in the old
nursery. All of us transcribing her words,
in turn, within the early pages of our
    draft biographies,

    the `one-two, one-two.`
The business of `the wave-break.` And how many
times have we heard `the little acorn` (a lapse
into kitsch—*die kleine Eichel*) drawn across
the floor by that wind-blown yellow blind. Her words
(her words!) are throughout these Gardens—she has
signed them so. We cannot simply describe
these places (can barely discern their colour,
their sound or shape) without first acknowledging
her own recollection of them. Only
then do they appear to us, like Chinese
paper flowers dropped in a glass of water.
They appear—just as they appeared to her—
    and we write them down.

Repetitively, like
a schoolroom punishment: `from the Garden,`
`the grey-green of it,` on the blackboards, the chalked
`pear-shaped leaves of the escallonia.`
In our workbooks, where the fishing boats are `caught`
`and suspended.` This stream-threaded, grey-green
Garden, where she has spent her entire childhood
as it now, late at Rodmell*, appears to her.
Here, where it is `always summer.` And, with night,
`always starlit.` This great Cathedral space
of Childhood Recollected, as she will
always have it: filled by her mother. The
ghostly incense of Julia, suffusing
    the windy, fishy, air.

*A 'Sketch of the Past'
Written 1939–40.

    Leslie, *paterfamil-*
ias, rests in his wicker chair beneath the
cedar (κέδρος), mouthing from his annota-
ted Plato's *Protagoras* (Πρωταγόρας).
He wears the summer jacket in white linen
and smokes one* of his pyramid
of pipes. Ginny, on the lawn nearby is
fully caught by the eldest of the 'writing'
Bröntes, with Rochester, back in England,
ignorant of the madness in his new
wife's family—her behaviours now blown
bestial: the crawling on all fours, the snarls,
the biting, the stabbing. Who has already
    set his bed to flame.

*The clay.

***

VIRGINIA STEPHEN

Mothing

At the first of late-
afternoon, the treacling of the lower
branches begins*. With dusk, the moth-catchers
return, lanterns in hand. A large moth (their
wish, a Death's-head) is feeding upon
the treacle, wings spread wide in ecstasy;
the crimson underwing aglow with lantern-
light. They uncork the wide-lipped butterfly
jar; closing it on '*Wild Moth-flutter*'; dust
smothering the glass, and to see it so
inescapably trapped, is a pity mixed
with mild disgust. The following morning,
Laura is out to lick the branches. Her large
head bent forward, face

wallowing in the
treacle and moth-dust. Her eyes raise at their
first approach: "*br-br-br*——" she essays, but can
get no further down the narrow passage
of its letters. "*Branches*," Ginny offers back.
"Sweet, hard branches, like Brighton Rock." She and
Nessa, scheme—imaginatively girl-to-
girl—upon their stuttering (honey-tongued)
half-sister fixed upon the bark. Breathlessly,
they catch her tongue within the jar, and take it
('*br-br-br*' it thrums) inside the house *to pin*.
Meanwhile, back in Laura's slowly working
mouth, the treacle seeps into the cavities;
and sets within the gums.

***

Time passes, and Jane
(now a woman of independent means),
returns to *Thornfield*. But what she finds there
is a blackened ruin: a shell-like front
perforated with paneless windows: no
balustraded roof, no chimney—all has
collapsed within. The story, she learns from
the inn-keeper.

*This method of moth-catching
was introduced to the Stephen
sisters by Jack Hills, later to
become (briefly) the husband
of Stella Duckworth.

"Mr Rochester's wife—a lunatic—was kept in the house," the host explained. "She had a woman to take care of her called Mrs Poole—an able woman, and trustworthy—but *she kept a private bottle of gin by her*. Now and then she took a drop over-much... and the mad lady would steal the keys from her pocket, let herself out of her chamber and go roaming about the house. On this night she set fire first to the hangings of the room next to her own, and another below, where the governess used to live. Then took off for the roof."

Ginny knows this ending.
The lunatic's hurtling shadow, flame-fed,
bent by junctions of wall with skirting board,
architrave, shuddering upwards, to the roof.
Rochester calls her name—*Laura*—even as
she jettisons herself into the flicker-
ing, crackling darkness.

Ginny marks her place
(towards the close of CHAPTER 36);
rises, and moves out into full sun, holding
within her tight-shut eyes the last moments
of darkness; bringing this blot of cedar-
shadow with her, ignorant of how it assembles
itself to her slender body's mass, in time
for it to be seen (to her opening eyes)
a natural enough phenomenon hardly
worth the mentioning.
                              In the Coffee Garden
she finds Stella organising groups for
photographs (*profusions of the escall-
onia* behind them) to be taken with
her new camera. But

in none of them do
we find a photograph of *Laura*. Ginny
writes of a tongue-tied, vacant-eyed and stam-
mering girl, `whose idiocy was becom-
ing daily more obvious`, and barely
mentions her again. No images of
swollen-headed Laura, with her heavy-
lidded eyes and other trappings of the
'moronic'. Loose-mouthed Laura, spitting out
her meat across the tablecloth. Laura,
hurling herself to exhaustion across
the lawns. In the biographies, Ginny's
half-sister is not like the *one-two, one-two*.
    And though she would have

VIRGINIA STEPHEN

been bound, in moments of
necessity (and drawn across the floor),
she is not cherished like **the little acorn.**
Laura is no *kleine Eichel.* The pre-
cocious Ginny watches her *half-sister*
swooping on the cricket pitch. Laura,
whose inner darkness is each day made more
visible. Laura, *half-sister,* who has
always been the shape of her fear. An embod-
iment whispering of a time to come. Not
physically, thank God; at least not *that.* But
should her own intelligence begin to cloud—
signalled, say, in a maladroit translation
    from the ancient Greek...

Some nights Ginny is
awoken by calls, a disembodied
howling (issuing from a room in the
distant west wing), so animal that it
gathers her body together in fright.
A half-hour of it, sometimes more, then
a silence—atrocious in its emptiness,
in its denial of the noise that has
preceded it; as if it sought to say,
what howling do you speak of? And then fills
itself with every manifestation
of snuffling and snorting; scuttling itself
along the corridor, towards her room and,
    mercifully, passing it.

***

Suddenly she finds
her feet relinquish earth. Her child-body* drawn   *between six and seven
up through the hallway's dark air (hands holding
her upper chest, beneath her armpits) and
stood on the ledge outside the dining room
where the servants rest the dishes (plated-
up, then empty) before (coming, going)
opening, closing the door. She stands there,
motionless, as Gerald's ^{18yo} hand moves
beneath her dress; **his hand approached my private**
parts* the fingertips trickling (as if in   *'A Sketch of the Past'
defiance of some Newtonian law)—*wrong,*
it is wrong to allow them to be touched—
    disgustingly upwards.

***

    Later, perhaps even
that same day, an afternoon when there is
silence, stillness, in the house, she returns
to the hallway: the ledge with its small looking-
glass. On tiptoe she can see her face, the
blushing-stain of violation rising in
her cheeks, her neck, suffused there by this single
glimpse. But surely she must understand the shame
of letting someone touch you? Surely she
must understand how simply standing on the
hallway ledge is an unpardonable *encour-
agement*. How close she lets us come to her—
this older Virginia, writing, late at Rodmell—
    only to have us find

    the dippings, scratchings,
of the nib (persistent as the waves that break
beneath our picturings) have paused. With each
especial feature fleeing from our knowledge—
the escallonia relinquishing its
hold on the fishing-boats: their presence no
longer *caught* and *suspended*, leaving our own
pointless imaginings of a sea: neither
deep blue; nor *emerald green*; not *purple*, nor
white-crested stormy grey. With some memories
striking her (as they strike us) as unlikely.
Could she, a child of seven, have lain in bed,
the Aristophanes in its ancient
    alphabet before her?

Laura's Teeth

During Leslie's bereavement following his wife Minny's [Harriet Stephen's] death, when Laura was no longer kept out of his way, he realises that she is not only slow, that her hands are not "obviously framed to grasp the pen", but that she may have inherited her grandmother's madness.

Laura cherishes
her teeth—the jagged, blackened, rocks of them.
Alone, she likes to roll her tongue within
the cavern of her mouth, drawing comfort
from the scenery she feels there. They are
still her best defense. When at night she hears
the bedroom door unlatch and discerns her
brothers entering (when she was a younger
girl, she mistook them for a single shifting
body) she holds firm to the bed, waiting
till they are all-but over her. And then,
and *only* then, she snarls, and bares her teeth
and puffs the mingled stenches of her mouth
    full in their faces.

To catch them off their guard,
she sometimes adds a fierce windmilling of
the arms, or else a grotesque facial gesture
(taken from her father's repertoire) and
other weapons as they come to mind—a hiss,
a serve of spit or, when her dress is lifted,
breaking wind. Eventually (they know), if
they persist, it will exhaust her; she will fall
into their outstretched arms*. Sometimes, garbled
through their laughter, they propose a marriage
and the necessary consummation. For
such fancy games they bring the *Veronal* and
force a triple-dose down her throat. She has
    descended into Hell.

*A motion they refer to as *Die Umarmung der Liebe*: 'the love embrace'.

***

Stairs

[1886] With lack of space making
Hyde Park Gate unliveable, Leslie orders
renovations based on Julia's designs ^{sketched on a sheet of notepaper to save}
^{an architect's fees} —converting the old attic into habit-
able space, adding a top floor[†] and install-
ing the house's first bathroom. On his own
volition, Leslie ^{at the last minute} commissions a second
set of internal stairs—this time in spiral
form using the clockwise configuration[††]—
rising from the basement to the new attic
landing. In the ^{ordinary run of things}
these were to be used by servants, despite
the spiral's perilous dimensions. When asked
as to the benefits of this ^{seemingly unnecessary} addition,
          Leslie would offer
a clouded sentence or two, based around some
of the following concepts—back-and-forths,
          the avoidance of creaks,
arrivals and departures, expedience,
invisibility, general timeliness,
          volte-faces, decampings...

[†] The Survey of London noted how the choice of 'two extra brick-faced storeys to an otherwise stucco-fronted building provided an obvious case of architecture mutilated by inappropriate additions'.

[††] That is rising in a clockwise fashion when looking up from the bottom of the stairs. Leslie's choices would have been based upon the usual design of the Mediæval castle—the clockwise configuration favouring the (usually) right handed defender who could strike, unhampered, downwards with his sword; whereas the right handed attacker, climbing, would have his sword-swing blocked by the wall. Inspired by this glimpse of history, at one stage the idea entered his mind to build the stairway from stone... but was swiftly sent on its way.

★★★

[1893] Eventually, it becomes too much for Leslie, Laura's fits, her babbling, her spitting, the thrashing of the arms, beating wildly at emptiness— hearing it (how could one *not* hear it!); catching glimpses of it from a window (the hectic rolling out across the lawn), or thumping down a staircase, only to thump back up the other. It disturbs his work on the biographies. And Julia, who has to care for her—he can see it wearing her down; coming home from hours of pastoral work (the poor, the ill, of England) to the sight of his idiot daughter, the racket of her, howling, shrieking. Her *fiendish* bursts of temper, her *dreadful fits of passion*. He has her admitted to **Earlswood Asylum**, where she is diagnosed as an 'imbecile', this being a milder type of 'idiot'; worse, though, than a 'moron'; with the 1901 census choosing to describe her simply as a lunatic.

***

EARLESWOOD
from Clinical Notes (1893–1945)

Mouth: puss-boil ulcerated cheek and lip... Very rotten teeth
and offensive tartar. Breath offensive... Collects saliva in her
mouth... Severe restraint required for dental examinations
and treatments... Suffers delusions of sight and hearing. At
times bellows and gesticulates... Shouts fragments of repeated
words without context... Bellows *Go away!* at any opening
door... Will spit out meat when eating... Is usually upset and
cries when visited... Restless and wakeful at night... Talks
wildly to herself... She is the same as ever, and never stops
talking nonsense and babble... Continues to spit out any solid
food... Occasionally says, "I told him to go away" or "Put it
down", quite sensibly; but the rest is incoherent... Temperature
still raised at night... Rambles on about boys and being in bed
or on the floor. At times shouts out and gesticulates... Still
hearing voices and talking wildly to herself. Mostly about
boys and her family... Still restless and wakeful at night.

***

    Having failed to under-
stand the fits, the howls and babbling, the thrash
of arms, and spitting of the meat, as *an-
other language*, all that can be instanced is
'ongoing incoherence'. For Laura,
inarticulate, *speechless*, half-sister,
born twelve years before Ginny Stephen, living
four years beyond, this torment can only
be dispelled by death—in the dark of the room,
this greater (two-headed!) darkness swaying
towards her, with its smirking voices and the
odour of stale urine rising to her face
from beneath the peeled-back foreskins of its
    two white English cocks.

Jem: A Brief Digression

Then Jem[†], again, in
the relentless pursuit of his Cousin
Stella, arriving at the door with his mad-
ness on him, to marry her. *My Star; Do not
expect to find a man worthy of your love.
No man can be really worthy of any
good woman's love. Nor any woman worthy
of a good man's. You are not worthy of mine.
And so good bye, my Star: good bye, perhaps
for ever to your lover, but never
till he died to you.* Jem, with his broad shoulders,
and his very clean-cut mouth, and the deep
voice, and the very blue of his wild eyes.

And with his madness.

[†] James Kenneth Stephen, known as 'Jem' by his family and close friends,
was first cousin to Virginia Stephen. 'Jem' was a King's Scholar at Eton
and at King's College, Cambridge. He was also known as a poet—his verse
worrisomely misogynistic and sadistic.

And his violence.
But Julia cannot shut the door upon him.
"I cannot shut my door on Jem," she says
to Leslie. But Ginia and Nessa have
devised a '*Wild Plan*'—one will intercept him
at the threshold, innocently enough,
to say "she's gone, I don't know where", the other
ushering Stella by the second spiral staircase;
hiding her in one of the new attic rooms.
Should Jem be encountered by mischance upon
a nearby street Kensington High, DeVere or Canning, Queens Gate Mews, they
[will say she's out of town—
"I'm afraid, she's out of town," they'll say. "She's
staying with the Lushingtons at Pyports."
But Jem, one day, frantic,

priapic, breaks through
these best-laid plans, and dashes to the nurs-
ery where he attacks a loaf of bread
with his swordstick (the moment ever after
talked about as Jem's *tilting at Breadloaves*).

On another occasion—the *'Wild Breakfast'*
episode—he appears at the family
table. "Savage* has just told me I'm in

*Dr George Savage was a family friend and Virginia Woolf's specialist.

danger of dying," he laughs aloud, "or
going mad"; those close to him attributing
his increasingly disturbing behaviour
to an injury incurred whilst horseriding
in Felixstowe[1886] in which he took
    a blow to the head

    by a windmill sail*.

*Quentin Bell suggests the injury was caused by a blow from 'some projection from a moving train.'

Stephen, still alive, but mad, commonly
gives Common Room recitals of his poems
at Cambridge. These ballads of barely disguised
rape are much admired; and fondly remembered
by alumni. But he is coming to the
end of his life.* And it ends quickly enough.

*Savage's prognoses proving correct.

(Coinciding with the end of verified
Jack the Ripper murders.)
                    Walter Headlam[†],
King's Fellow, author of *Lapsus Calami*,*

*Slip of the Pen.

a book of parodies and other verse,
founder of the TAF* Club (of which Stephen

*Twice a Fortnight.

was a member), receives an urgent message
    from Jem's landlady

[†] Later involved in a flirtation with Ginia during 1907.
Headlam died of an accidental twist of an intestine in June, 1908.

    to come quickly to
his lodgings, where he is discovered at
the opened bedroom window, naked, singing,
whilst engaged in a fervent defenes-
tration of his belongings. Dr Savage
(who will shortly treat Ginia's breakdown with
similar enforced confinement) recommends
that he be admitted to an asylum—
St Andrew's Hospital—in Northampton.
As in his previous two years, Jem's behaviour
swings between depression and violence. He re-
fuses all food and rest; and within three months
of his admission has successfully
    starved himself to death [1892].

        ***

The Last of Talland

She, who has fallen,
awaits her expulsion from the Garden.
But quite inexplicably, she is
permitted to remain. She is still allowed
to walk beside, amongst, them—the passion
flowers, the calla lilies, the masses
of escallonia-blooms with their crimson
honey-fragranced flowers, the large-leaved purple
clematis—jackmanii, the fig marigold
with its showy pinks or whites opening
only to the sun. Here, yellow flags, and
at the top of the oval, bright-eyed purple
African daisies... No, six years will pass
    before the banishment.

    It happens slowly,
but (as she will look back on it) with an
inexorable accumulation.
There comes a Year [1894] bringing with it a sequence
of reversals, of lesser unfairnesses
and injustices, all gathering to the
great calamity. Early that summer it
begins, in their second week of holidays
at *Talland*. It is Ginny who hears the first
disturbance, rending the tranquility she
has always known here. The rending of child-
hood. The rending of all continuities.
She follows the noise of it, down, passing
    through the wooden gate,

    stepping down the rough
stone-block steps, out into Albert Street. As
she pulls-to the wooden gate behind, it comes
to her that soon there will be no return:
they are bringing down the house that lies
immediately below them on the hillside.
The pale grey Cornish slate—*scantle slate*, as
it is called here—stained with golden lichen,
is being dragged to the ground, whole rafts of it
reduced to rubble. Unsalvageable.

She visits the clearing site every day,
till only the red-and-white-potted chimney-
stacks remain; these last moments, teetering
    on their fireplaces.

    Leslie makes enquiries.
A hotel. It will be a hotel. His speech
an almost-sung lament—a tremolo
baritone—single-noted, in rapid
reiteration. The *Porthminster*, he says
and falls silent. At this mention of the name,
his anger rises. A *grand hotel*, he
starts, exaggerating every syll-
able with derisive clarity, rolling
the *Grand*'s 'r'. Three storeys high. Taking from
them their coastal view and, with it, unforgiv-
ably, the lighthouse on Godrevy Island.
In Ginny's room, the blind* stirs slightly. All   *which is no longer yellow.
    within, blank, pointless.

                    ✳✳✳

    For Ginia, nearing
thirteen, the moment she has long awaited
has arrived: *this*, her fall from grace. Another
garden grows before her eyes in the shadowed
spaces of the terrace. It comes to her
how this is not so much expulsion from
The Garden, as that—without warning—an-
other garden has inexplicably
overrun it. The years in Eden are lost.
By the first week of October, the weather
has already turned, the view glimpsed through the hedge
is filled with grey sea, flecked with white. Julia
returns to London, carrying this grey-
    flecked sea within her.

                    ✳✳✳

    In Autumn, [1894] (from her
voluntary nursing) Julia contracts
rheumatic fever. And, inconceivable
as the loss of the view from *Talland*,
so she slides unsalvably to her death.

A late family photograph* (given her
conspicuous absence from the tableau,
taken by Stella) shows her mother, (seated,
barely able to support her own corpse-weight)
pallid, thin-lipped, hollow-cheeked, her eyes skewed
sharply to the right, beyond the frame, meeting
something of which the children are quite un-
aware. In May [1895], with Spring ubiquitous,
  abundant, she dies[†].

*Wimbledon, 1894.

[†] In *To the Lighthouse* (1927) Woolf borrows much of her parents' lives
for the Ramsays. Mr. Ramsay (she famously writes within square brackets),
stumbling along a passage one dark morning, stretched his arms out, but
Mrs. Ramsay having died rather suddenly the night before, his arms, though
stretched out, remained empty; inviting comparison with a late memoir of
her mother's death: "...early on the morning of the 5th of May 1895... George
took us down to say goodbye. My father staggered from the bedroom as we
came. I stretched out my arms to stop him but he brushed past me, crying out
something I could not catch; distraught". ('A Sketch of the Past', 1940). What
was it that transpired between Ginia and Leslie Stephen in that darkened
hallway—her distraught father staggering from the bedroom, 'brushing past'
his daughter's outstretched arms? Or her distraught father, arms outstretched,
oblivious of his daughter, running towards his wife's death bed? Or was it that
Ginia arrived in the hallway to witness her distraught father, emerging from
the bedroom, running into the hallway's darkness, his arms outstretched. In
Suspiria de Profundis, De Quincey (one of Julia's favourite authors) speaks
of the temptation of suicide when 'we stretch out our arms in darkness'. Was
it that Lesley Stephen hurtled forwards, oblivious of his younger daughter's
presence, in search of an embraceable void, "whilst, George led [Ginia] in to
kiss [her] mother, who had just died".

  Leslie does not fling him-
self upon his spouse's grave as Julia had
upon her husband Herbert Duckworth's—lying
there, inconsolable, wretched, for hours.
Instead, wearing his usual dark suit, black
gloves and cravat, with the addition of
a mourning handkerchief*, Leslie, arms out-
stretched (eager to embrace the darknesses
which may appear at every corner) still glides
above the corridors and stairs, finding flights
he never knew existed. Till, it strikes him
that this wife is dead—with so many duties
to be done; so many spaces filled with
  histories of Great Men.

*that is, black bordered.

***

A numbness enshrouds
Ginia. She feels nothing when she stoops
to kiss her mother's still-warm face, which, the
following day, is `like cold iron`. At
22 Hyde Park Gate, rooms are now shut.
The hallway reeks of flowers—prominently,
lilies, (for was not the Virgin Mary's
tomb once covered in this flower?), but amongst
them, gatherings of rose, *white* rose, of hya-
cinth, hydrangea. The summer holidays at
Talland will be discontinued. Leslie rages
at *Porthminster*, as if it were culp-
able of Julia's death. The simple *saying*
    of the word disgusts him.

***

    But how could a man
retain his sanity, alone, amongst so
many memories? The *pear-shaped leaves of the*
escallonia. The balcony, where his
wife... Even here (a whole country's width away),
he is wracked with them. Meanwhile, at such a
distance, the emptiness of *Talland House*
prepares itself to enclose others—such as
Scottish painter Thomas Millie Dow*, who   *1848–1919.
leases *Talland* after the Stephens—the life of
    whom does not belong here.

***

    He thunders through the house,
in `extraordinary dramatisations`
`of self-pity`, slamming every door behind
him; bellowing his misery, such that one
might well think the place an abattoir. Other-
wise, he `sits spectacularly with his`
`head on his breast`. The visiting Florence
Bishop, at the afternoon tea-table re-
marks on how he is looking `remarkably`
`well`. Nessa takes the ear-trumpet and con-
veys her comment; he is insulted. He should
be receiving her sympathy. The trumpet
is transferred to Miss Bishop who withdraws
    `her unlucky remark`.

And this question asks
itself: who is there with strength to carry
this family, this husband and these children,
to lead them through that dark amalgam known by
the syllable they speak aloud as *grief*?
Gr ie f: syllable of three syllables—
soft growl, high keening, wind-stroke moving back
into wind. Who to hold these children, mother-
less. This husband, without wife? For he is brok-
en by it—his every moment eaten up
by anger, or these shrillnesses of loss,
this disappearance of every substance
                    into air, wind, smoke...

More Stairs

Perhaps as part of his
madness after Julia's death, Leslie now adds
a third ^iron *staircase*, cleaving ^in a zigzag to the outer wall
at the rear of the property; providing
access for the passageways at every
level of the house, except the attic, or
brain, as Ginia calls it, of the house's
body: her father's library and study,
where now he sits at the centre of the room
in his rocking chair (a writing board set
across its arms), lamenting the terrace's
inherent absence of side walls[†], either
of which would have allowed for the future
        construction of *a fourth.*

[†] No 22 shared a common wall with the terrace to its left (as seen from the
street); to the right it was separated from its neighbour by the narrowest of
lanes.

VIRGINIA STEPHEN

Missbrauch Haus

22 Hyde Park Gate,
then, possessed neither the refinement, nor
the cleanliness, of a geisha house. Rather,
it fostered the crudity and the animal
imperatives of a brothel; its staircases
—with their range of ingress, egress, points—
clearly facilitating such a function.
Could Leslie have possibly thought this at
the time of their commission; might it
have risen through his clouded consciousness
as a form of architectural Freud-
ian slip? What does seems clear is that after
Julia's death it becomes *ein Missbrauch Haus*—
   a house of abuse.

***

Stella

Between the bellowing,
the roars, the groans; between the oaths and beat-
ings of the breast, Leslie, ravenous for
attention, his need for sympathy grown ill-
icit—lets fall, in gasping half-sentences,
the details of what he expects of her.
Ginia, closest to Leslie, to madness, to
the coarse desires of men, standing in the
drawing room's darkness, knows too clearly what
he seeks to voice. Knows how the *thought* of it
emerges incrementally (*unthinkable*
in its full unveiling); his grief's terrible
extortion: that Stella ^{at the age of twenty-six}, must take upon
herself the thankless (*impossible!*) task
   of *being* Julia—
fulfilling every duty that she had dis-
charged. An unqualified self—surrender
   to her stepfather's needs.

***

The Getting of Wisdom

    At (just) thirteen, Ginia's
knowledge of sex was based upon Plato's
deliberations on sodomy; and the
violation at 6 years-old by the 18
year-old Gerald Duckworth. Now (its advent
facilitated by Julia's illness
and death), Ginia is visited by
the elder [36yo] Duckworth. Eton* & Cambridge   *Member of Eton First XI.
educated, George, (we find him snuffling in
the *dramatis personæ* of an early,
unfinished, novel*—`sentimental, pompous,`   *circa Sept., 1902.
`utterly unintellectual`—and,
in subsequent recollection*—`his small brown`   *'22 Hyde Park Gate'.
    `eyes perpetually`

    `boring into something`
`too hard for them to penetrate, but which,`
`on a pig, would allude to something ob-`
`stinate and pertinacious... as if he`
`were grouting for truffles and would by sheer`
`pertinacity succeed in unearthing`
`them`—enters Ginia's bedroom, whispering
"Don't be frightened. And don't turn on the light,
oh belovèd. Belovèd—". Possessed of
an animal urgency, running loose on
the roses eiderdown, he flings himself
pillow-wards; his small-eyed, faun-eared, sharp-toothed,
mustachioed, truffling face pressed close to hers;
    enraptured. Conjugal.

***

                                          VIRGINIA STEPHEN

An Unexpected Arrival

Violet Dickinson:
contented spinster of Quaker background;
for a year, the Mayoress of Bath; author
of essays on *the happiness of spinsters*,
and the disadvantages of being six
foot two. ("Nurse, bring me the weighing machine," said
the doctor. "It's the foot rule you'll want, sir," said
the nurse.) And here she is, striding down the hall
at Hyde Park Gate... *tall, plain, and ramshackle.*[†]
A photograph [1902] shows her a looming, softly-
smiling presence, embraced by a barely
recognisable Ginia now twenty years
of age. How old this young woman looks, how
haunted, how frail—a frailty we have seen be-
      fore in later photo-
graphs of Julia. The posture, though, belongs
upon a *lost*, defenceless, child clinging to
      its mother. Sadly,
we have no image of Violet's barrister
brother Austen (Ozzie) Dickinson's az-
      aleas from which
Edward [VII] famously shouted obscenities;
and amongst which biographers* still forage   *from 1904 onwards.
    for the seeds of truth.

[†] But an observer who would stop here, putting her down as
one of those cleverish adaptable ladies of middle age who
are welcome everywhere, & not indispensable anywhere—such
an observer would be superficial indeed. (Virginia Stephen,
"Friendships Gallery" (1907)

End of Part One

ANDRÉ BRETON
IN MELBOURNE
(1942)

Breton at Sea

André Breton,
     Surrealist
the large head of him
the pale face upon it, angry
the graceless body of him
     Breton, his tread heavy on the sidewalk
     Breton, dispirited by New York and its barrage and its emptiness
     Sulking, Breton,
     with Jacqueline *thriving* there, speaking increasingly in English
(such odium!)
     Jacqueline, preposterously, *painting* now!
     Jacqueline, with her lover pandering to her every affectation
     Breton, his marriage in tatters
(what of *l'amour fou* now?)
     unable to either work or write
     in desperate accordance with the laws of chance
and upon receipt of a letter of invitation
     from a Gino Nibbi of Melbourne, *Australie*
     Breton, large-headed, pale-faced, his features spread
across the expanse of it (like pegs to the canvas of a tent)
     Breton, hair swept back
his long wide tie flowing from the stiff collar, flung
     across the shoulder of his suit,

LEFT AMERICA

                           travelling by train to
Mexico, where he spent some weeks eating burritos
with Diego Rivera, and where, on as many occasions
as practicable, he visited the grave of Trotsky with its
emblem of the two crossed picks and the inscription:
AMOR VINCIT OMNIA.

    From Mexico he took an open-sided bus to Panama
where, since the time of de Lesseps (A man, a plan, a
canal: Panama) it had become the habit of the locals
to communicate wherever possible in palindromes; a

situation intolerable even for a Surrealist. He stayed at the Hotel de Lesseps (*Içi on Parle Français*— shortened to accommodate the felicitous palindrome, *Içi*) in a double room with bath, the water of which would mysteriously fall and rise. The almost universal adoption of the palindrome made ordering food in restaurants especially onerous—the challenge of working, for instance, a simple crepe with tomato and a little cheese, into such an arduous form, left him exhausted, with all appetite gone.

Frustrated, embittered, malnourished, Breton bribed passage on a packet boat bound, via several Pacific islands, for Australia. As with many Frenchmen before him, the fetishes of Oceania called, as did the unlikely fauna of his destination—the platypus, the kangaroo, the bunyip not to mention the indigenous savages (the twins of which race he had heard possessed telepathic powers) and the large red rock which formed the hub of the entire continent.

His heart went out to the *San Romano*, as the boat was called, and he referred to it affectionately as his "little ark"—this floating city with its walls of iron and its oceanic moat. He would spend hours watching the funnel feed its smoke into the skies as if it wished to join the weather; or watching the negro sailors demonstrate how to tie elaborate knots in rope. He would walk up and down the metal stairways clacking his shoes like a young girl in taps. But most of all he enjoyed standing at the prow of the boat staring out towards an empty horizon, which gave him the delicious sensation of movement without progression.

"Ah, the relentless momentum of stillness!" he would exclaim to passing crew members and clap his hands together.

Poetic images began once more to spring into his head and he would record these immediately in the small black leather notebook he had purchased in Panama to assist in the construction of palindromes. Breton grew particularly fond of the stops for the picking up and delivery of mail. The shining negroes carrying away the sacks and returning with others, like robbers bringing home their spoils.

So the boat zigzagged its course through the Pacific Ocean, chugging first to the Galapagos and then the Marquesas Islands, reaching Hawaii—where the American Fleet stood so proudly—by the middle of the first week of December. At night he would be lulled to sleep by the strains of "Camptown Races"—sung in unison by the homesick negro sailors—drifting to him through the porthole window, carried on the soft warm air.

Back at sea, a day out from Hawaii, Breton, clacking at the aft of the boat, made out on the horizon a gathering of terrible darkness. A storm, he guessed, of prodigious strength, in which clouds heaped themselves one upon the other, until there was a curved citadel, black-hearted. Hopefully, he thought, his boat would continue to out-run it. At night though, he returned to the rear of the boat and looked out anxiously to where an astonishing medusa-head of lightnings intertwined themselves like a bonfire of thin light on the otherwise *grand noir* of sky.

The *San Romano*'s next landfall was Samoa and thence to the Phoenix and Solomon Islands. It was at this time Breton came upon the idea of charting the course on his copy of the Surrealist Map of the World. As, perhaps, a direct consequence of this (for what other explanation could there possibly be?) islands mysteriously began to amass and to disappear to the astonishment and consternation of the crew who, for example, would be confronted by shorelines hundreds of miles in excess of the islands they had visited many times before. The Bismarck Archipelago, for instance, was now a group of major islands easily exceeding the size of India. Breton's map and glass were confiscated and the remainder of the journey via the British-French Condominium and New Caledonia passed without incident. Indeed, they would be in Australian waters by the end of next week, the Captain informed Breton over a game of *Conditionals*.

Breton at the Windsor

Shortly after three in the morning the French Surrealist, André Breton, propped up in his bed at the Windsor Hotel, fell into a deep sleep in which he dreamt himself back in Mexico with Trotsky (in whose skull the ice-axe was still embedded). The revolutionary told him that over the thirty or so months since his death he had been working through their earlier co-authored manifesto on the relationship between art and revolution (there was, he bemoaned, so little otherwise to do) and that he had come up with a revised and significantly extended version which should now be offered to the world.

Waking in a trance-like state, the revolutionary's face still before him, Breton became dimly aware of his own hand (clearly impelled by a force outside himself) reaching to the bedside table, feeling for the fountain pen, then returning, crab-wise, purposefully, to the bed. Trotsky's distant wavering voice began dictating the new manifesto—Breton could quite clearly hear the sound of the nib scratching, sometimes sputtering slightly, at the uncommonly resistant paper; and his eyes took in the ink-spattered page expanding by some miracle to accommodate the flow of words. So he worked slowly on through the hours before dawn. Until even as he wrote out the last word of the last triumphant sentence the spell finally relinquished its hold. Breton took one single breath in the world of reality and fell back into a deep dreamless sleep.

It was just before nine when he raised himself from his bed, surprised to find that neither sheet nor blanket covered him. It was then that the memory of his earlier awakening came back. He slid from the bed and, wiping his eyes, looked down at the place where he had lain. The page that had grown to accommodate the text now all too obviously revealed itself as the under sheet. The handwriting, though perfectly legible, was barely recognisable as his own—understandably, given its origins and the resistance of the linen (Such a phrase, it struck him: "the resistance of the linen"). But beneath it all, was his own clear signature, and below that, conferring on the document an unarguable authenticity:

***

"It is chance alone which is capable of rendering account of the effects of the blind *mêlée* which now shakes the world."

Breton met the faces of the artists (and the poet, Harry Hocking) who had gathered round his table at the Leonardo.

"Everything conceivable is possible," he continued. "And everything possible tends toward manifestation, so that whatever is represented tends to be manifest. Nothing can appear in the artistic vision that does not elaborate itself and gradually become the phenomenon of the future. Which accounts for those efforts so noticeable in totalitarian governments to restrain, at all costs, the spirit of discovery, of invention in art."

Applause.

During which Breton found himself gazing across the room to a far table where an attractive dark-haired woman sat writing what appeared to be a letter. This was clearly the same young woman he had noted at the Leonardo the day before when he had agreeably supposed she might have been writing to him, and found himself for the remainder of the day awaiting her letter. Naturally, nothing.

Now here, at nine thirty, on the morning of January 15th 1942, she once again assumed that attitude— looking at the ceiling, the pen, a wall, her gaze never meeting his own. For Breton, during those precious moments, the room became free of any other presence; as if a wave had swept away the artists to whom he suddenly found himself still talking.

"Even though all external liberty were abolished," he was continuing (it was an argument he had expounded many times before), "that inherent, fundamental liberty, which gives its sole authenticity to liberty itself, will be concentrated, more directly than ever before, on works of art, in order to take life by surprise."

Warm, enthusiastic applause.

"This message of the future (that proof of the insatiable desire leading to the verge of discovery; that continual surpassing of what has already been attained) can never be lost, even though it is transmitted, for the time being, underground. It assigns to man a role entirely contradictory to that which, at this time, the masters of Europe wish him to play. But this message still breathes; and most vigorously in those countries—like Australia—which remain free!"

Vigorous applause.

At the end of which Gino Nibbi, the *Padrino* of the Leonardo rose, as if to propose a toast (surely cups of coffee were not appropriate). But it was *not* a toast, merely Nibbi rising to say—

"The only necessity in art is that it shall continue to express itself..." He paused. What was the word he needed? And the characteristic silence began, and increasingly within it came the irritated gasps and the grunts of frustration. The Italian's hands began a ferocious windmilling until he declaimed:

"...to express itself *imperiously*!"

Breton had noticed the woman from the moment she had first entered the bookshop and ordered a *macchiato*—with the "merest stain of milk", she had said—and, having chosen the table at which she now sat, distant from, but facing him, she had reached into her bag and removed a sheaf of stiff paper, so uncommon in a time of war. He had heard its quality the moment her nib began to move across its surface; and he noted how the scratching was not dissimilar to his own efforts earlier that morning.

Cheering. Applause.

The sudden outbreak of noise brought Breton's attention back to the conversation.

"Thank you," he said, and nodded his head humbly. "Originality, ever greater originality in art, must be sought as the supreme antidote for the poison of the times in which we are living," he offered.

"Indeed," said Nibbi, standing. "As Hegel said—in art everything depends on the liberty with which the imagination succeeds in bringing herself, and herself alone, to the centre of the stage."

He sat.

"And was it not Baudelaire," said Breton, "Who told us—be it heaven or the abyss of hell, one must plunge into the heart of the unknown in order to find the new."

"Who can forget the words of Rimbaud," added the Italian, standing, "One must always be absolutely modern."

"Nor can one forget the prophetic words of Franz Marc," added Breton, "In the twentieth century we will live among strange men and faces, new images, and unimaginable noises."

He looked up, beyond the faces of the artists, beyond the corpulent figure of Nibbi, desirous once again to observe the mysterious woman; but she was gone. Only the empty table, with a small, empty, *macchiato* glass, and in the air the faintest stain of perfume where she had most recently passed by.

***

Having knocked twice on the door and received no answer, Viola Cookson backed herself into Room 123, her trolley with its supply of brushes, dusters, polishes, disinfectants and the like, pulled behind her. Secure now in its emptiness, she began to clean the room, the procedures of which were eccentric, possessing, as she did, an aversion to dirt generally, and a morbid fear of human waste and its traces in particular. Her first act always, unless a tempest raged beyond, was to throw wide the sash windows and let unbreathed air flood into the space. Done, she proceeded immediately to strip the bed. Eyes squinted, she gained her bearings, then, with her lids tightly shut, her hands gloved (in fact she wore her gardening gloves) she reached out, wrenched the soiled linen from the mattress and bundled it into the laundry sack.

***

Back at the Leonardo the conversation had shifted to the war—in particular the advance of the Japanese.

"...which will founder at Singapore," declaimed Harry Hocking.

"The invasion of Australia by the Japanese..." enquired Breton, "is such a thing possible?" His eyes glancing down at his watch as if they might arrive before lunch.

"If they get past the British, it's very possible," said Strachan.

"And that's an opinion held by a lot of Australians," added Sidney Nolan, joining the conversation for the first time.

"*Too* many for mine," Strachan added, "and I'm English."

"The simplest solution would be for everyone to become a Surrealist," Breton advised. "On the Surrealist Map of the World, Japan does not exist. It is *L'Île Pacques*—how do you say it, here?—Easter Island? Yes? It is Easter Island which dominates the Pacific."

"On what basis?"

"On the basis of their *statues*, of course!" came Breton, indignantly.

"Well, if Easter Island attacks," said Strachan, "I feel bound to say the British will be taken completely by surprise."

***

Breton climbed the last steps of the large carpeted stairway which led to the first floor rooms of the Windsor, his conversation with Nolan still drumming in his ears.

As a matter of courtesy, in a lapse in the conversation, Breton had enquired of the young Australian what he was working on at the present time.

Nolan, who more than anything else had been captivated by the largeness of Breton's head, was caught unprepared.

"Everything's a bit *Entre deux guerres*, as they say, at the moment... but I *have* been thinking of doing a series of paintings about Ned Kelly."

And Breton had leaned forward, his wide brow deeply furrowed, and asked, "Ned Kelly? *Qui est-ce?*"

If Nolan had not happened to be carrying a series of photographs of Kelly wearing his armour the conversation might have ended there. But Nolan had pushed aside several empty tasses, reached into his bag, retrieved a number of photographs, and laid them down on the table like a winning hand of cards.

"Who *is* he?" Nolan replied to Breton's enquiry. "I would call Kelly a *revolutionary*."

Breton looked down at the photographs and was astonished. The helmet with its eye-slit reminded him immediately of the African masks he had seen in Paris in the 1910s and '20s. The armour was nothing less than an expression of a more primitive form of the surreal. It was as though the ancient continent of Australia possessed a kind of subconscious dreaming which surfaced in revolution through the surreal images of Kelly's armour. Or could it be that one continent dreamt the other? And he saw instantly how the surreal could be universally at the service of, and essential to, revolution.

He had left the Leonardo in a state of near ecstasy. First the manifesto, and now this! The day of January 15th 1942, he said to himself, would surely go down as one of the most important dates in the Surrealist Calendars of the future!

Back at the Windsor, he inserted the key in the lock of his room, opened the door and strode inside.

***

"It was there. In my room, this morning, not more than two, perhaps three, hours ago," bellowed Breton, continuing the conversation with the desk manager he had begun on the telephone only minutes before. "I visit the Leonardo for a decent *café*. I speak there for a time with its proprietor, a Mr. Nibbi and several Australian artists—in particular with Sidney Nolan—a painter, perhaps you know of his work?—on the subject of the famous Australian revolutionary, Ned Kelly. When I come again to the *chambre* it has been cleaned. The manifesto is not there! It has totally disappeared!"

"I never saw a manifesto," stammered Viola Cookson, having no idea what such a thing might be (her mind conjured up a type of snake) but galvanised by the knowledge that, even with her eyes squeezed shut, to miss such a thing would have been impossible, if the snake *had* been in the room.

"You see, Mr Breton," the desk manager said, adopting a tone of finality. "We have it—as we say *here*—'from the horse's mouth'; *de la bouche du cheval* as you might say, (relishing his schoolboy French which seemed to be returning to him by the minute)— manifestly, there was not a manifesto amongst your sheets."

"It was not *in* the sheets," Breton raged, exasperated by the man's continued missing of the point. "Do you not understand? *Le drap est le manifeste! Le manifeste est le drap!*"

"Thank you, Viola," the desk manager said to the maid, "that will be all." And he signalled her to return to work. Viola scurried back, glad that the French had chosen not to colonise Australia.

"I obviously need to inspect the sheets myself."

"I'm afraid, Mr Breton, that is not possible. All our linen is handled by Chang's—the Chinese laundry. This morning's despatch—with or without the item in question—was collected over an hour ago."

"Then I must ask you, as a matter of urgency, for the address of this Chang's Chinese Laundry! *Donnez-moi l'address! Vite! Vite! L'address, monsieur, immediatement!*"

The desk manager wrote the information on a slip of hotel letterhead and passed it across the counter.

"I shall telephone," he said, "and let them know you are coming."

But Breton was already on his way.

The desk manager glimpsed him pushing through the revolving doors and then, when he had attained the street, saw him run off at full speed. *À grande vitesse*, he thought, a little more of his French coming back.

***

Chang's Laundry had been built on the site of an abandoned temple from the early days of the Gold Rush and incorporated much of the original building. It was to be found in a lane off the eastern end of Little Bourke Street.

Breton pushed his aching legs onward. His tread heavy on the paving stones. He could see all too well the sheets (frail, so frail), the inks boiling from the page, dissolving into the water, the sentences unravelling in foam, the last ghost-trails of their passage tumbling through the lightless drains out into the bay to lie, no more than the faintest of stains washed up on a further and a further beach. So that as he stood on the stock-block steps which led to the laundry—his clothes awry, his hair deranged as Tanguy's—he felt his quest had already failed.

In despair, without reason for hope, Breton numbly pushed his way through the doors to find himself in a room whose size (though it was clearly not a small room) was difficult to gauge on account of the pervasive cumuli of steam. It was as if he were walking through the sky itself. From these clouds, obscured in the near distance, a voice called to him.

"Monsieur Breton. Monsieur Breton."

Perhaps, it suddenly occurred to him, the exertions of running had caused him to have a seizure of some description and that he had arrived in Heaven. His attacks on the church in general and on Mauriac in particular now struck him as far less witty. He moved tentatively forwards, in the general direction of the voice, which called him again—feminine, high-pitched, and now (a face was emerging from the dense vapour) identifiably Chinese. The likelihood of Chinese angels was small and he felt immediately more relaxed.

"Monsieur Breton," said the (*young*, as he now saw) Chinese girl, who was dressed in ornately patterned silks of red and gold. "You are here about the sheets?"

"*Absolument*," he replied, mopping his wide brow, but wholly heartened by this first evidence of competence. "You see, there was some—"

"Follow me, please," the young woman interrupted, handing him the end of a fine silken rope and she moved off into the clouds. Breton felt the rope tug in his hand and he stumbled after her.

"Mind the steps," came the girl's voice not long after. For suddenly there appeared a considerable number of them; a broad staircase-full, leading upwards, slowly rising above the steam-clouds where the girl was finally revealed, waiting with the other end of the rope in her hand.

Behind her, dwarfing her, set in a wall covered with intricate red and gold lacquer-work, was an entrance way composed of two prodigiously large mahogany doors.

Above this doorway, in relief (the rest of a massive wooden beam having been carved away) was a single Chinese character.

"What does it say?" Breton asked.

"Sheets," the young woman told him. Then, "Mr Chang will see you straight away," she added and bowed. Breton stood rooted to the spot, a little overwhelmed by the unfolding of events.

"Please," she urged, pushing back one side of the double door—effortlessly, it appeared—and inviting the poet to enter. Breton stepped forward. Once inside though, he came to an immediate halt, for the room he had entered seemed to be like an ocean which was flowing towards him, a huge vertical tide, in wave after wave of white. He turned to run, but the door had already been closed against him.

He stood, eyes squeezed tight, waiting for the first of the waves to crash upon him, to crush him against the doors. There was, however, no crash, no crush. Indeed, the only sound the writer could hear—once the throbbing of the blood in his ears had abated—was a whispering, soft and low: a sound of wings, flock upon flock, myriad, floating as if on high; the only sensation the laving of a warm wind against his face and his feebly outstretched hands.

Slowly, he opened his eyes.

The view was as he had remembered it—and he flinched once more against the torrent. But nothing. Just the huge tide of white, somehow halted in its breaking. Wave after wave of white. Rippling, it now became clear, from the ends of suspended silver wires. Breton found himself to be in an immense corridor (if this word were in any way appropriate to the enormity of it—even in the *châteaux* of the Loire he had never seen anything on this scale); a long wide corridor flanked on both sides with white sheeting, lolling, shifting in the gentle breeze. Through the midst of this billowing ran a single straight aisle, down which Breton began to walk in the face of the soft wind, as though he were walking along the spine of some prehistoric white-winged bird. As he moved past the hung linens, two things became obvious: first, that their size varied considerably—from those suitable for the covering of marquees, those for the making up of beds, through those of tablecloth size, down to those one might carry neatly folded in one's trouser pocket; second, that each of these squares, large or small, had upon it (from a length appropriate to an essay to the meagre syllables of a haiku), *writing*.

Breton continued down the aisle until he became aware of a distant figure, a seated Chinaman, he hazarded. As he drew closer, he was proved correct, though one signal feature had escaped his eye—a pigtail of extreme length and agility which coiled serpent-like about his head, its plaited strand, ready, it seemed, to strike out at any moment. Breton halted.

"Mr Chang?" he enquired.

The pigtail turned to face him; then, like a slow after-ripple, the man himself.

"I am André Breton," the Frenchman announced, "the world famous writer and founder of Surrealism. *Sans doute* you would be aware of my autobiographical novel *Nadja* and, more recently, my masterpiece on *l'amour* and *l'irrationalité*, *L'Amour fou*."

"Monsieur Breton," came the reply, delivered with the intonation of certainty and in a Cambridge—King's—accent. "How delightful to meet you. I know *Mad Love* well—the image of the Chinese lanterns slowly catching fire among the chestnut trees will stay with me for ever."

***

"Oh, there is a very long history of linen-writing in Melbourne," Chang explained. "A number of major writers have visited this city and left a mark of significance upon their sheets, if not the corner of a table-cloth." And he began a litany of names: "Trollope, Kipling, Mark Twain, Conan Doyle, Joseph Conrad—"

"Conrad?" questioned Breton.

"Yes, indeed. Whilst in Melbourne, Conrad wrote a short story, an addendum if you like, to *Heart of Darkness*—"

"In which?" urged Breton.

"In which the river connects via a subterranean passage to the Paris Metro system. One makes a *Correspondance* at Châtelet."

"Ridiculous!" Breton spurted, dismissively. "Quite preposterous!"

"I admit, the first time I heard of it, my reaction wasn't dissimilar to yours. But I have since learned that once you are fully underground everything becomes potentially close. *A throw of the dice abolishes distance*, as Mallarmé scrawled on a table napkin at *Le Bateau Ivre* restaurant, a souvenir carried back to Australia, *par hazard*, by Christopher Brennan." He sighed. "Yes, so many works—from the bloodied miseries of Lawrence's handkerchiefs to the pillowcase poems of Rimbaud."

"*C'est incroyable!*"

Chang drew the poet closer.

"In July of 1876, after deserting from the Dutch Colonial Army somewhere between Batavia and Semarang, Rimbaud made his way to Australia, staying some days at a boarding house in Port Melbourne from which he sought passage back to Europe."

"But this would post-date *Une Saison en Enfer*."

"Indeed it does," said Chang. "Of course the great majority of Rimbaud's fugitive writing remained stored in Hàrar—the manuscripts were far too cumbersome to be carried with him across the desert to Zeila, though he packed a few shorter pieces knowing they could double as bandages in a crisis. The bandages are now kept by the laundry which services *L'Hôpital de la Conception* in Marseille. The great bulk of his linen-work may be found in Yap's Chinese Laundry in Djibouti."

Breton shook his head.

"So, you say he wrote *poems*, not just invoices, in Hàrar."

"Most certainly. Rimbaud never once abandoned

the idea of himself as a poet. Why else would he choose to keep the 1890 letter from de Gavoty of the literary review in *La France Moderne*, which referred to him as 'the head of the decadent and symbolist school'. Be sure of it, poetry remained with Rimbaud to the very end.

"Yet for all of this," Chang continued after a breath, "I am forced to admit that the most astonishing documents kept in the sheet halls come from the hands of those yet to be discovered—as Alexandria contained, for instance, numerous plays by Greek poets which totally eclipse the brilliance of Aeschylus, Euripides or Sophocles—the terrifying *Pit of Ruin* of the Syrian dramatist Khar Oubed, for example: a work of which is it said that not one of those who dared see a performance survived more than a third of its length (actors were permitted to appear in no more than three of the thirty-three scenes) causing the manuscript—written on several tent canvases—to be enclosed in a massive lead-lined box."

Breton stood a moment then slowly turned to face the linen. There, lapping before him, was the living evidence of dream intermingled with reality. And he came to understand how there could easily arise another literature (another art) which might thread a passage between sense and nonsense.

"I cannot understand why these things have never seen the light of day," said Breton. "The whole notion of what might constitute literature would have to be rethought." (And, he imagined, along *Surrealist* lines.) "Why has no-one spoken of this before?"

"Because those few who know of their existence also realise that silence is their best chance of survival. As you would know, from time immemorial libraries have been sacked by the barbarian—both old and new—burnt to cinders. Had these books remained hidden from all eyes they would still exist. Ah, the sorrow of the librarian!"

"How many such halls are there?" asked Breton, in growing awareness of the enormity of his discovery.

"There is hardly a city in the world which does not contain a linen collection," explained Chang. "Except for those countries in which the Chinese are despised or seen as the enemy—for such places would be particularly vulnerable to desecration at any time.

"And you must appreciate that not all of the holdings are works of literature. Many artist's sketches adorn the linen-halls of the world. From the expected— Lautrec tablecloths, for instance—to the astonishing. The Chinese laundry in Rue Mouffetard in Alexandria, for instance, contains an ancient shroud which shows the *back* of Jesus' head.

"But this is hardly a concern for us today, Mr Breton. *Today*, your manifesto has found its way to the library. This is excellent news for both of us... but it is not without a certain problem."

"A problem?"

"Let me explain. All linen-work is produced in some form of ecstasy. The impossibility of maintaining a trance-state for any great length of time accounts for the general absence of novels, five-act plays, epics of any description... other than the work of Khar Oubed— which makes his achievement even more astonishing. Most authors remain unaware that they have even produced such things—for their visions are often well beyond the scope of their previous imaginings. Kipling's contributions, for example, are startling— often resembling the outbursts of old ladies under anaesthetic."

"But I still fail to see a problem."

"Obviously enough, your own experiments with automatic writing, dreams and the unconscious, have permitted you to be simultaneously aware and unaware. Others merely wake in a semi-trance, find they have ruined a sheet, immediately bundle it into a drawer, or cupboard, and quickly leave the hotel in order to avoid a bill!

"But you, Monsieur Breton, *you* are different. It is that difference which places you in the position of having to make a difficult choice."

"Which is—?"

"Which is whether you take your sheet with you, or whether you decide to leave it here."

"There is no choice!" declaimed Breton. "Could any

true revolutionary immediately make of his manifesto a museum piece! This sheet, Mr Chang, will become the flag of artistic upheaval! The torn and bloodied banner of all true artists throughout the world!

"Besides, Trotsky's signature alongside my own is the vindication of automatic writing as a revolutionary tool. The authority of the document and the technique depend upon it."

"I am glad your choice was so simple to make," said Chang. "For others I'm sure giving up the opportunity to hang here in the hall of the sacred wind, billowing alongside the linens of Rimbaud and Mallarmé would be difficult—"

"I would of course be perfectly happy to bring the sheet back after I'd shown it to a chosen few. A small exhibition perhaps. A—"

"But that would not be possible," said Chang. "None of these works can be on loan from the collection, even for the shortest period. There can be no exception. To accede to your request, or that of anyone else, places everything in jeopardy. For a library such as this to exist, it must not be seen to exist. Nor any like it, anywhere. Immortality, though, is the reward for silence."

Immortality, thought Breton. *Amongst the pillows of Rimbaud and the napkin of Mallarmé.*

"I sympathise with your dilemma," said Chang to the poet's silence, watching his anguished regard. "But, if I may say so, have you not all your life sought the gold of the times—*l'or du temps*? For indeed you now stand amongst it, here, drawn from hotel rooms and restaurant tables of this city and ultimately of the world—for all time."

For all time. How that phrase attracted him.

"Your concern for art and revolution is admirable," Chang continued. "And the signature of Trotsky is beyond doubt a valuable imprimatur. But after all is said and done, does not the value of an idea reside in its wisdom—judged by its efficacy in the real world—and not by its signatories?

"You may need to suffer the indignity of seeing these ideas attributed to your name alone, but the road of art is ridden with sacrifice."

"Yes," said Breton, the burden already heavy on his shoulders.

"Might I suggest you transcribe the passages of greatest insight, of greatest persuasion. Then go forth amongst the peoples of the world speaking their truths, content in the knowledge that the original, in its perfect form, lives forever in one of the halls of linen."

Mr Chang approached, the manifesto gently draped across his outstretched arms. Breton received it in his own, holding it there, savouring its weight; noting on the hem the words, inked deeply, indelibly—

Property of
The Windsor Hotel

—just as his mother had written his own name in her roundly infantile hand upon all his washables: shirts and undershirts, bloomers, handkerchiefs; writing such that he could all but feel the letters embarrassingly harsh against his skin.

"I shall return with paper," said Chang.

***

Two hours later, Breton strode from the lane onto Little Bourke Street, a transcription of the manifesto folded in his jacket's inside pocket. He had chosen to appear amidst the great visionary writings of the world. He had chosen immortality, and the sacrifice had enlivened him.

The Frenchman began to make his way back to the hotel, a different man from the one who had run so desperately those hours before through the streets of Melbourne. He caught his passing profile in a shopfront's glass. How Apollonian he was. Hair swept back. Bearing upright, regal. How astonishing that everything—Trotsky, Kelly, immortality—should have happened in a city such as this. On his return he would make a point of revising his Surrealist Map of the World to incorporate a much larger Australia. One far bigger than Easter Island. One that might justifiably occupy a substantial proportion of the Southern hemisphere.

Meanwhile, the young woman from the Leonardo was about to reappear in the street—the face he had frenziedly feared never to see again was there, and so close, turned towards him, that its smile in that moment left him for all time with the memory of a squirrel holding a green hazelnut.

She told Breton she had written to him. The letter he had seen in Nibbi's bookshop and café was destined for no-one else; she was surprised no one had given it to him. And, as he was totally unable of thinking then how to detain her, she rapidly said farewell, giving him a rendezvous for that same evening at midnight.

***

With the manifesto still folded in his jacket's inside pocket, Breton strode westwards along Flinders Street towards the famous Railway Station. The meeting-place that the young woman had chosen was perfect—what were the row of clocks above the station entrance if not the simultaneous vision characteristic of surrealist looking? Their range of times abolishing all feeling of duration and conjuring an intoxicating atmosphere of *chance*?

The poet, with the suffering joy of the pursuer, found himself understandably buoyed by his unreasonable optimism about love, and the impossibility of an answer. He came to a stop at the corner of Flinders and Swanston streets, the great surrealistic edifice looming from the darkness. The steps of the entrance were, however, indisputably empty.

How perfect was her absence.

"To possess is no longer to love," Breton declaimed in excitement. "The truest love exists in pursuit alone. Everything must lead to the *next* time, which is always 'for the first time'. Endless pursuit, yes, with the *possibility* of resolution."

With that, two burly men emerged from the pervasive darkness, took him by the arms, and escorted him to a nearby car.

Mina Loy

A Shorter Life

L loy d

1

> There goes Haweis, the artist in
> his twitching cape, ascending the
> staircase to an assignation whilst below
> Mina Loy births their second child.

But the Florence Years [1905–15]
have seen them both take lovers. Besides,
he'll end up like all her seducers—in a book,
not well disguised (homophone, anagram)
whispering, as though it were the first time
uttered, of grey-blue eyes. Of black hair,
centre-parted. Hair which, un-loosened,
would cover her thighs.
      Take Marinetti.
Fascist. Woman-hater. Up all night, with
his friends beneath the mosque lamps,
now perpetually dramatised in *Pamperers.**
confined there with his yearning for mud;
gulping at the factory drain and dreaming
 of his nurse from The Sudan.

*A theatrical satire about the Futurists, written by Loy, 1915–17: published in *The Dial* LXIX: 1 (July 1920)

2

 Yet for Papini, his ugliness
fostering timidity in affairs of the heart,
she writes *Love Songs* of white villages white dawn
and dusk. Unthinkable the white of smoke from
their house. Only, he resents her time with
Marinetti. Dear Mabel, she writes, don't
live to see a man sob out his rival's name in
the ultimate embrace. Papini, naked before her,
his nonchalant sack of flesh—a duality of
voluptuous and shrinking fragility. All the white-
nesses unmelding to the dross of his seed. Goodbye,
he tells her, for this evening and this life. In her
own sex war, intercourse become collision.
 Love, the parasitism of the weak.

3

Meanwhile, [Avenarius] Lloyd, now
Arthur CRAVAN, arrives in Paris,

> Paris, roped city, with your padded
> corner *portes* de Pantin, Neuilly, St Cloud, Bercy;
> Paris, with your streets of canvas;
> Paris, city raised four feet above the ground;
> the whole world looks up to you and
> watches your poems unfold.

                              announcing
himself as poet, boxer, nephew of Oscar Wilde
and painter of the imaginary canvas *World
Champion at the **Whorehouse**,* by which he means
the Salon des Indépendents. `Take Laurencin` [he writes]
[in Maintenant] `that mistress of Apollinaire – there's one`
`who likes a man to lift her skirts...`

After his release, Cravan (latterly, defamer, ex-
prisoner), gives notice of a lecture at *Noctambules*,* *A café-bar, 24 boulevard de
après ça he will kill himself with an overdose   Clichy, Pigalle.
of absinthe. `For the benefit of the ladies,` he
appends, `I shall deliver the lecture in a jock strap`
`   and place my balls on the table.`

4

[February, 1917] and the New York
Evening Sun votes Mina Loy the exemplary
'modern woman'. She can write free verse and
paint lampshades. She can act, design her own
sets and costumes. *She can tell what Futurism is
and where it comes from.* This woman, they say,
*is already half-way through the door into
Tomorrow.*
        In the meantime word comes of
Arthur Cravan, now Fabian LLOYD, grandson
of the Queen's Chancellor, man of fashion,
chemist, acrobat, camel, sailor, thief, peasant,
bourgeois, millionaire [He is all things, all men and all]
[animals!] recently embarked in the city with
    introductory letters from Picabia.

5

Mina first sees him in a photo-
graph (primly seated on a chaise longue,
dressed in a three-piece suit with spotted tie
and matching socks, his hands placed
demurely across two Siamese cats). The first
she meets of his *fatal plurality* are gathered
in ^Walter Arensberg's studio; all of them 6'4",
dull, sullen, in respectable tweeds. And each
of them a devotee of Hugo.
                              Shortly after—
at Grand Central Palace, clambering to his feet
to deliver a lecture on 'Independent Artists
of France and America'—Cravan disrobes and
bellows drunken obscenties to the audience,
   till detectives drag him off.

6

Yet she cannot rid herself
of the sight of the towel turban wrapped
about his head. The way it gives his face
the significance of great sculpture. Shortly
afterwards the modern woman comes across
her surname firmly held within his own. Finds

      ^Fabian L LOY d

Colossus ^(her apartment can barely accommodate sculpture
^on such a scale), she susurrates (*monstre*, lovely
as Venus), close to him, Colossus, Great White
Hope, `it is not given to each of us to be desired.`
He is thirty-one and tenderness awakens
in his Colossus body. `A deluge of luxury`
   `a weak man could not afford.`

         Then without warning the American FIRST
         WORLD WAR begins. Perfectly disguised as a soldier,
         Lloyd absents himself from New York City.

7

Mina, meanwhile is half-
way through the doors at Webster Hall exiting
a gathering[†] The Blindman's Ball, **May, 1917** into Tomorrow
(3.00am, to be precise) leading a *ménage*
à cinq to scrambled eggs at the Arensbergs'
and thence to Duchamp's four poster bed,
where they lie in a loose cubist arrangement—
a naive precursor of Modernism.

LLOYD, (now once again CRAVAN), writes
from Mexico asking for a lock of Mina's hair.
Better yet, he says, bring all of your hair. You'll
love it here - the stories they tell about bandits
are all lies. Telegraph me from the border.
    I want to marry you.

[†] Ultra Bohemian, Pre-Historic, Post Alcoholic.

8

CRAVAN has become Professor
of Boxing at the *Escuela de Cultura Fisica*.
Soon there will be a Match [September, 1918] over
20 Rounds against Jim Smith [(Black Diamond)]
for the Championship of Mexico.
                              Cravan sits
in his corner on a chaise longue. His shorts
and socks are fashioned from a spotted material,
as is the loosely knotted tie about his neck.
At the sound of his name he leaps into the ring.
Announces himself as boxer-poet, acrobat,
muleteer, hunter, monkey... Jim Smith, who
says nothing, wins by a knock-out in Round 2.
Vale the 'Professor'. *Voilà, Le Début de*
    la longue marche pénible.

9

They move village to village.
They eat strange fruit which ripens and rots
in one minute. They feel it move in their
mouths even as they swallow. They travel

past roadside shrines, rich with paintings
of local miracles. In Guadalupe, Mina paints
the dark-skinned *Virgin of St Teresa*'s leading
Colossus down from the pantheon to be married.
Cravan organises boxing matches held in jungle
clearings—squares with no trace of vegetation
bordered by taut horizontal vines. In Oaxaca*,   *wə-HAH-kə [English
where Cravan is victorious in the ring, she paints   pronunciation]
a tribute on the shrine to St Pugnacious,
     Patron Saint of Boxers.

   10

Les Saisons de Boxe

Each night, she stares
upon the damaged
body, watching

shallow pools
of bloodrush rising
from below the skin.

         A deluge of luxury a weak
         man could not afford.

Over the days they flower
and re-flower there,
red-blue and green,
yellow, golden-brown.

Spring of blooms
Autumn of leaves
reduced to Winter's
white flesh.

   11

    One over-mooned night,
finger-tracing her shoulder blades, Cravan
finds several vanes with white barbs and a floss
of afterfeathers, like the seed of dandelion.
He soaks a portion of her hair (which, un-
loosened, would cover her thighs) in water.
He wrings the hair, gathering ink from its

blackness. After he has garnered sufficient for
the task, he rolls Mina on her side and tugs
gently on a shoulder feather, swivelling
the hollow shaft, easing it away from the
follicule in her skin. He dips it in the *encre
de cheveux* and begins ^{in third person} the final chapter of
  the story of their lives—

```
        Mina is pregnant, and this is no place for
        pregnancy. Using money from his victory in
        Oaxaca they travel on the Trans-Isthmus Railway
        to Salina Cruz where she takes the one remaining
        berth on a hospital ship bound for Buenos Aires.
        The remainder of the winnings he spends on a
        small yacht. A season later, he sets sail for
        Buenos Aires and is never seen again. At night
        his dead words of amour drift back to Mina.
        She, condemned to muteness, knocks out messages
        to him on her bed frame. She eventually returns
        with their child to Europe. She spends the
        weeks on board looking out across the surly
        leaden sea.  AC
```

12

Envoi: Paris

*An Asterisk is the signal of a treasure which is not there. Its absence
is secret and potentially powerful; for others it is an empty wordlessness
only obliquely aware of its unfulfilled promise. My Dear Mina
writes Natalie Barney, I am so grateful for your book.
It put me in mind of an evening at my salon.
A jazz-band supper, sometime in 1927
it must have been, where you read *un poème
inédit*— '*la Veuve et le Jazz*'—and you ex-
claimed: husband, how you cuckold me
with death. What became of it, the poem?
Yes, she can recall the brutal sear of jazz;
with desire receding to the distance of
the dead. COLOSSUS, she calls to this horizon,
  the sullen whiteness of the page.

                              *

Reports

Less than a month after Cravan's disappearance, the first of the reports appeared, with the boxer-poet being sighted in the gold-fields of Durance. Shortly after, a rumour spread that he had been stabbed to death by bandits; no body had been found—only a bloodied (now-empty) money-belt laid out upon a stretch of sand. Mina's favoured explanation was that he languished in a Mexican jail, a belief so strongly held that she returned to Mexico in 1922, making an exhaustive, yet fruitless, survey of its prisons and their inmates.

The following years witnessed a slow but regular stream of information on Cravan, mostly in the form of new aliases. The most persistent of these were claims that he had been living under the name of Dorian Hope (the forger of Oscar Wilde manuscripts); or the reclusive B. Traven (author of *The Death Ship* and other Mexican novels—at the time supposedly in a Swiss sanatorium). Other aliases to emerge included both Felix-Paul Greve (German poet and novelist) and Frederick Philip Grove (Canadian novelist). Later studies in impersonation/impostorship have suggested Cravan had been masquerading as André Gide's secretary in the period between the disastrous publication of Corydon in 1924 and the writing of Gide's only novel, *Les Faux-Monnayeurs* (1926).

***

sentinel
in an unknown dawn
strewn with prophecy.

¹⁹²² She conceives a novel
of Colossus, his extraordinary life;
and their cruelly-short time together.
But how convey the richness of those days?
Colossus, incomparable being,
whose holy speech was all-but **impossible**
(not to mention **dangerous**) to express?
Would she be condemned to approximations?
Impoverished recollections that could only
magnify the nature of her loss? But from
every *souvenir*, she gleans profundity.
Prophecy. Was it not Colossus who fore-
told the horrors of the **Great War** with its
incomprehensible loss of life?

Was it

          not Colossus who
declaimed an aesthetic (falsely attributed
to the monocled Romanian poet?*)   *Tristan Tzara
          of a new beginning—
not of *art*, but of *disgust*? And she conjures
an image of him, sentinel outside
          the Hippodrome with
his wheelbarrow full of *Now*†. So it is,
she ascribes her knowledge of the present
          to earlier pronoucements
by Cravan, lending them the force of augury...
of myth. For with his absence, what was left
          but to reinvent him? ††

---

† *Maintenant*: Cravan's scurrilous and totally self-authored magazine—
a clear precursor of Dada—which he sold from a wheel-barrow parked
outside racing tracks, art galleries, sports centres and the like.

†† See Loy's description of her parting from Cravan as given to Julien Levy,
below—a situation never existing outside of her imagination.

***

As For Poetry

          she drafts *Anglo-Mongrels*
*and the Rose** Of high skies coming gently upon her   *A sequence of poems
and all their light shining out of her—(indissoluble bliss to be   1923–25
carried like a forgetfulness into the
long nightmare). She makes for herself a New
Family. **Exodus**, the father Jewish Hungarian and
Ada the mother English Christian, bequeath to their un-
gendered child, **Ova**—born a clotty bulk of
bifurcate fat—a mongrel identity.
Her fragmented race, religion and language
cannot help but create a new *mongrel-speech*
(with its fragmented diction and syntax);
an affected, mannered, deliberately
artificial language suited to what
          Europe had become.

Interlude
(c. 1924)

Every Thursday, at the *Transatlantic Review*'s new office (an old domed wine-vault with a grey view of the Seine below the Quai d'Anjou), Ford Madox Ford holds teas for his assistants, contributors, and sundry acquaintances. Ford edits from a birdcage-like gallery at the top of the vault—so low, he reminisces, that I could never stand up straight. Hemingway preferred to read manuscripts out on the quai.

One of Ford's assistants is the young and barely published poet Basil Bunting[‡]. Bunting (not long in Paris) has been appointed secretary and sub-editor of the *Review* solely on the cognizance of Ezra Pound (himself, not long in Paris) who has described him as the finest of prose stylists in the world; though it should be mentioned that at their first, and recent, meeting Bunting had confessed that Pound's *Propertius* was the finest of modern poems.

Stella Bowen, Australian artist and appointed tea-maker, looks up, to see her husband—tightly framed by the semi-circle of arched roof—rise, head lowered, slowly from his desk. Presently, she knows, he will descend, spreading geniality amongst the faithful. In recent times, the centre of attraction at Ford's Thursday teas has been Mina Loy (not long in Paris)[‡‡], five years on from her husband's disappearance.

Immediately captured by her dark and melancholy beauty, Bunting approaches the couch on which she sits, announcing himself as conscientious objector, escaped prisoner, editor of Major Harry Barnes MP's *Valuation & Revaluation for Poor Rate and Income Tax, Post War*, artist's model, international drunkard, and poet.

Do you box, Mr Bunting? Loy enquires.

Not as such, he replies. Though I have on occasion brawled.

He amuses her, this 'old-fashioned Englishman' with his dreadful Northern accent; and she urges him (from amongst his list) to take the call of poet the most seriously—causing him to fall at least half in love with her. He sits, unhappily, listening to her talk of Cravan—this sudden rival who enjoys the insuperable advantages of being **young**, having been **lost-at-sea**, and most probably being **dead**.

From a position nearby, Laurence Vail ('King of Bohemians', husband of Peggy Guggenheim, Dada painter, sculptor, and will-be author of *Murder! Murder!* a satire on his—failing—marriage[†††]), listens to Loy's monologue: its `excessive self-absorption;` `its tiresome rehearsal of her catastrophes.`

[†]Bunting will go on to international fame, in particular for his long poem, "Briggflatts", 1966.

[††]Loy's collection of poems, *Lunar Baedecker*, its title misspelt by the publisher Robert McAlmon, had appeared the previous year.

[†††]Begun c.1926, published in 1932. In Vail's novel, Mina Loy will appear as Miriam—although `notorious for her sympathetic attitude` `towards unusual strangers, attractive waiters, pittoresque` `beggars, sweet drunkards, she has little respect for the` `misfortunes and enthusiasms of her friends. Yet, can` `one blame her if she is unable to extend her notorious` `sympathy to those bores who think their catastrophes are` `worth her own?`

***

The Time of Lamps

Poetry now arrives
piecemeal. In its stead she turns, as she had
in New York [1917], to the assembling of lampshades.
Every Sunday finds her at *les marchés*
aux puces,* of Clignancourt filling her basket   *the flea-markets
with old liqueur bottles and a mix of plugs
and switches, sockets, bulbs and flex. The shade
panels will be made from discarded maps,
papers, cellophane and other translucent
materials—the dross of it rendered
luminous. `When you go to Mina's apart-`
`ment,` Sylvia Beach remarks, `you thread your way past`
`lamp shades that are everywhere.` But they *attract*
such interest, that Peggy G. is offering
    to back her venture—
purchasing a shop [1926] for a *lampisterie*
in rue du Colisée [No.52] a narrow street
    off the Champs-Elysées [8e].
The building is *une pollution visuelle*.
Mina & Joella* will, of course, need to   *Mina's eldest living child
                                          to Haweis

do the repairs* and
renovations themselves. In preparation
for the opening, without telling Mina,
        a range of underwear*
has been draped between the lamps (as we then
thought to make some money) giving to this
        night mosque an intim-
ation of the brothel. This upset Mina
so much [Peggy G. relates] that she refused to be present
    at the vernissage.

*dismantling partitions,
fixing the widely-cracked
enamelled walls.

*fashioned by PG's mother's
seamstress

***

She's telling Levy[†] all
about it now [1927], at a party in Laurence
Vail's studio, *tout près de* the *lampist-*
erie itself. She attracts him (if you
recall, with his own [elusive, beautiful] mother dying when
he was seventeen); he is fully taken
by her beauty, her elusiveness. Mina,
mind, at forty-four still looks young. Exception-
ally young, almost blond...
                    A FEW MONTHS BACK,
in New York, Marcel Duchamp had persuaded
would-be writer Levy to join him on
a voyage, by sea and train, to Paris. Bob
McAlmon's* going to be aboard, he notes.
    And probably Man Ray...

*American author, poet
and publisher of Loy's
Lunar Baedecker
[as McA. will misspell it].

    At six o'clock, with
Levy unpacked-and-sorted in the Mc-
Almon-recommended *Hotel Istria*
(Marcel will say the same [McAlmon had said]. He's lived there.
With Man Ray's studio right next door—the man himself,
McAlmon—not Ray, nor Duchamp—arrives to
take Levy to a party at Laurence Vail's.

    In the background, conversations spiral
out from Pound and Hemingway; from Stein; from
Cocteau and Colette. Against a far wall,
Isadora Duncan—living tableau[††]—
engrossed by her increasingly excessive
lifestyle, *drunk*, occupies far more than the full
    dimensions of a couch.

[†]Julien Levy, son of Edgar Levy, NY Real Estate Mogul, knows a little of Loy—the most recent example being her poem "Brancusi's Golden Bird" which was reprinted in the sculptor's exhibition catalogue at the Brummer Gallery where Levy and Duchamp had first met in 1926. It is likely he would also have read Loy's earlier poems in *The Dial* 73 (July and November), 1922.

[††] 'Living', that is, only till mid-September when, a passenger in an Amilcar CGSS, her overly-long hand-painted silk scarf becomes (famously) entangled in the car's open-spoked wheels and rear axle. From here, reports vary, with the entanglement either: (i) pulling her from the open car and breaking her neck; or (ii) hurling her 'in an extraordinary manner' from the open automobile and instantly killing her by the force of the fall to the stone pavement; or (iii) with the sudden tightening of the scarf strangling and almost decapitating her. On hearing of her death, Gertrude Stein remarked how "affectations can be dangerous".

But Levy's gaze remains
on Mina Loy (`almost blond, because her`
`bobbed grey hair holds so much vivacity`),
who has, as usual, drifted into the
telling of Cravan; with Levy, totally
unaware of being caught up in this
sticky legend she has spun around herself.

She is creating for him a favourite scene
in which the `child-criminal`, boxer-poet,
Colossus, sails away in a small, poorly-
repaired yacht into the Gulf of Mexico
leaving her—pregnant—wrapped in his overcoat,
waving farewell from the shore... A spell broken
only by the sweeping entrance of `the most`
      `wonderful jeune fille`
`in the world`[†], the twenty-year-old Joella,
`like light breaking through the clouds of cosmo-`
    `politan chitchat.`[††]

[†] McAlmon's opinion...

[††] and Levy's.

Chez Natalie Barney

And so we arrive
at the evening of May 6[th 1927], a Friday,
early in Barney's *Spring Salons*—a jazz-band
supper given in honour of Mina Loy.
For her, it conjures an earlier* smoke-
filled—*jungled*—room, where she had sat, listening
to the brute-angels in their human gloves.
It *undoes* her, this *Africa.* Her white
flesh quaking at the brazen dissonance;
forcing her, impelling her through the crowd,
glimpsing Levy as he rose from the table
in pursuit.
                    Outside, the threatless Gallic
air halts her, spins her into Levy's arms.
He hails a taxi [rue Jacob to her apartment], staying till the trembling
        subsides, then makes his way
home to the *Istria.*
                    Now, the jazz has
followed her here. Once again the raised metal
        trunks (O Monstrous Growth!)
are threatening to overwhelm her, as they *would,*
had not her hostess ended all their blaring
        and backfiring. And,
hearing her name aloud, Mina, threads *les
invités* as though angels were already
        nibbling at her heels.[†]

[†] Natalie Barney's description. Cf. Djuna Barnes who is at the salon to collect
material for her *Ladies Almanack.* She will cast Loy as Patience Scalpel, the
novel's only heterosexual, whose ankles are nibbled by cherubs.

***

She will read just one
poem, just-completed—'The Widow's Jazz';
having spent two hours earlier in an ante-
chamber, training * (as might a boxer, perhaps?)
for this moment. And in retrospect, how apt,
this reappearance of the jazz musicians.
The white flesh quakes, she begins, to the negro
soul, hearing a voice, strangely inflected, yet
familiar, moving out into the room. Then, in
the same breath, as they say—and as they *will* say—

their guest of honour is crying. Now, she is
calling out; barely registering the faces
of her audience rearranging in disgust—
    for their honoured guest is
howling like `a birthing cow`. Lacking all
propriety. *And here*, and from a woman
        of her class.
    `Cravan`,
                    she calls
upon him,
    `colossal absentee`
        expelling this grief—Monstrous par-
    `Husband`
turition.
    `how secretly you cuckold me with death`
        The voice (*mongrel*-accented[†]),
    bellowing in this
suddenly unpeopled space.
                  Berthe [Cleyrergue], back
in the kitchen with her emptied platters,
    is busy making
more of her `little sandwiches`...[††] `and God knows,`
`there were plenty of them`... `and they were eaten`
    `very quickly`. Whilst
Fabienne, Mina's eight-year-old child to
Cravan, stalks the room, seeming to Levy `some`
    `mythological beast`.

[†] German, is it? No, English? After all she is English born, though England
has never called to her. The pronunciation, intonation, is *mongrel*—the
English woman with her jostling blend of American (New Yorker), and
Austrian (from Haweis).

[††] Triangular in shape—`folded up like damp handkerchiefs`.

Developments

Edgar Levy, having carefully read William J. Burns (of William J. Burns Detective Agency)'s report on Joella Synara Haweis Levy Bayer (1907–) and finding no obvious impediment, books a berth on the first available liner to France. In *Paree*, he meets his prospective daughter-in-law and her *goddam attractive mother*; and agrees to his son's marriage on the understanding that Julien enters an apprenticeship in his New York real estate business as assistant supervisor of building construction. Julien and Joella wed in Paris August, 1927 and, following an extended honeymoon, settle in New York. For the first ten years of their union Mina calls them her children; but she remains flattered by her son-in-law's attentions.

The Time of Lamps

CONTINUED

1

At first, the keening—
the persistent, single, wordless voice, high-
pitched (at the extremity of soprano,
yet neither woman, man) waking her, at four.
Following its siren-call, manoeuvring
the meaningless foldings of her *peignoir*,
concerned, but without fear, still cursing the
undifferentiated silk, down the hall
to the *lampisterie*... she traces the lamentation to
a lamp single, luminous. What has *upset** it so? Then, even   *This being the actual word
as she looks down, the patterns on the shade-   which comes to her mind.
cloth (of a butterfly, a rose), both grow
fainter it seems , but in truth (with tired eyes) it's hard to tell
if this is so.
            With the blessing of clear light,
        she returns to the shop-
front, to the now-extinguished lamp, to the
soft pale leather of its panels. Gone though,
        the rose, the butterfly;
as if both had opened (petal, wing) and
taken flight... finding in their place—a row
    of meaningless numbers.

2

By year's end [1928], Mina is
living in rue Saint-Romain [6e], an *appartement**
acquired solely from the sale of lamps (sans
underwear). But sadly, with Joella in
New York, the shop has exhausted her. How much
easier it had been with her daughter's comm-
ercial bent, her ease with women from *Soci-*
-ety. `I am the most godforsaken`
`creature in Paris,` she scrawls on a torn-
in-half invoice plucked from the waste-paper
basket*. (Cravan had once said [she recalls] she was `too`
`bright to have friends...` and isolation only
leads to lunacy...)

*Nº 9, in the same building
as Djuna Barnes.

**corbeille à papier* (f)

And then lunacy
of a kind, appears. In the form of Monsieur
      Charcot, Loy's accountant,
who sends her figures of declining sales; and
she is gripped by fear (see her clutching herself),
      that her staff have sold
the technique of her Calla-lily lamp
to glassblowers; that lithographers now
      profit from images
of antique maps (those misshapen coast lines
endearing in their speculations: a Gu-
      jarati chart of
Aden's Gulf; a rendering* of the ocean's bed;
and *dozens* more) that she had unearthed over
      years of Sundays at
les marchés aux puces de Clignancourt. In short:
EVERYONE SHE KNEW WAS STEALING FROM HER.
      Till, one spring afternoon,
strolling the Boulevard Haussmann, she discerns
a bed-lamp's barefaced likeness in *Printemps* [a window display]
    at scarcely half-the-price.

*by Alexander Supan

3

Moments Décisifs

or

Suddenly, A Lot Happens

1930 It comes down to this: a ^monthly^
cheque from Julien Levy now funds the AILING
LITTLE LAMP SHOP OF COLOSSEUM STREET.
In the meantime, Peggy G. is telling
all her friends `It's simply not a viable`
`investment now.` `Besides, there's limits to one's`
`generosity...` But *juste à temps* ^as the French say^, or
just in the nick of time ^as do the Americans^, another cheque ^a loan^
^of $10,000^ arrives, this time from Julien's father ^Edgar^. Loy
buys out Guggenheim and, shortly after, sells
the business ^for 75,000F^. Now the phone is ringing—
it's Julien ^long-distance^—he's opening a gallery
in midtown Manhattan:[†] Would she act as
    his commissioning agent in Paris?

[†] The *Julien Levy Gallery*, 602 Madison Ave, opens November 2, 1931—in
the process launching the *press release* and the *cocktail party*. His first show is
a photography retrospective, including works by his friend and mentor, Alfred
Stieglitz. Levy quickly discovers that photography is not easy to sell, and
turns his attention to works of (mainly) European Surrealists—Dalí, Ernst,
Ray, Giacometti, Tanning, Magritte, Kahlo, Ray, Cornell and, notably, from
spring, 1946, onwards, Arshile Gorky. As she had been to Mina, Joella brings
her indispensability to Julien, building on her roles at the *lampisterie*, and
increasingly taking charge of hanging exhibitions.

***

A Grey Young Man

    Late in the year ^1931^ of
its opening, `a grey young man`*(over-
coat, complexion) visits Levy's gallery,
late in that grey November's day, close to
closing. From his pocket he brings a collage
on a cardboard mount—a *fin-de-siècle*
woman being sewn together on a ^sewing^
^machine^ table. `Would you mistake it for an Ernst?`
he asks. `I would` `almost` `think` `so,` Julien
Levy replies. `The` `precision, yes; and`

*Levy's decription in his
Memoir of an Art Gallery
(1977).

```
the understanding of what can and can't
be matched. But you need images that are
entirely yours... adding ᵂʰⁱᵗᵉ⁻ᵐᵃᵍⁱᶜ ʷᵒʳᵈˢ, why don't you try
working in the round? Maybe add some motion,
        some mobility.
```
He describes two photographs—one of a man
with a gun, another of a partridge;
        how they could be pasted
at opposite ends of a shadow box.
```
You could build a sloping alley. And let
        a bullet or a ball
bearing roll between them. And
```
he disappears into the storeroom, returning with some antique French
boxes he had purchased years before whilst picking through the stalls at the
Clignancourt *marché aux puces* with Mina Loy.
                              With the autumn
light all but gone, the two men part. In Levy's
        hand is the grey young
man's name and address, neatly written there
on a slip of paper: JOSEPH CORNELL,
    3708 UTOPIA PARKWAY Flushing, Queens.

***

OELZE
AN INTERLUDE

Julien Levy makes one of his periodic visits to Paris—consulting with
Loy on her latest acquisitions for his gallery. Whilst there, he accompanies
her to Clignancourt foraging in the *flea markets* for watch parts needed by
Cornell for his latest boxes. Before returning to New York, Levy asks Mina
to make contact with Surrealist painter, Richard Oelze.

1

    whose most recent address
was not yet a season old but had proved as
obsolete as had Levy's original.
Oelze (she learned that first afternoon) had
arrived in Paris March, 1933 from effectively Hitler's Germany
on the last train before the border closed.
Since then he had moved from apartment to
apartment, locations with a single
commonality—closeness to a railway
station.

Now the weather has turned blustery,
at every cross-street shouldering her, such that
on occasion Mina feels she is held to
the paving solely by the weight of her
    voluminous fur coat.

2

The door opens on
a tall balding man dressed in an evening suit;
a man of concave torso, his face `almost`
`luminous from starvation`, who speaks to her
auf Deutsch. She replies in kind; with her *mongrel*
origins, German is a familiar tongue.
It is enough for them, this brief exchange
of speech and of appearance, to know they
share a fundamental understanding
(`clochard to clochard`) `of those who are`
`fated to failure`. The `madwoman`*, in her   *Die Verrückte
fifteenth year of grief. The `madman`* with no food,   *Der Verrückte
anxious to sell a painting to buy himself
    a set of false teeth.†

---

† In particular, Oelze feels his options at a local brothel are curtailed by a
mouth filled with rotting stubs. Mina will soon find his teeth are not decayed,
so much as *worn* down.

3

She watches this man,
younger than herself by eighteen years*, still dressed   *Mina æt fifty-one.
in an evening suit†, brush-in-hand, his ashen
face with its array of bruises. She has
only recently noticed their presence.
(Does he slap himself in some misguided
self-disgust? Is such an occurence totally
out of the question? And if not him, *who*,
this mysterious assailant?)
                        As months pass,
it becomes clear this fiercely independent
man cannot exist as painter, as *person*,
without a witness to that existence;
only able to mature in another's
    imagination.††

† As Loy notes, via her novel, *Insel*, Oelze has an evening suit, but
never an occasion to wear it, so he puts it on when he paints
his pictures.

†† One night Oelze confides how he sees himself as a character from a Kafka
tale: starved, reclusive; hounded by circumstance. In Kafka (he says), I
found a foreshadowing of my existence.

  You atrocious fake (she replies), can't you see, you have no
life of your own to be written — you are acting Kafka!

  (To which he replies, in kind) And I see clearly into you. Your
brain is all Brontë.

4

Their shared life admits
no sexual intimacy. Loy thrives
upon the lovely equilibrium
that his companionship conveys to her.
For his part, Oelze lives at a distance
dictated by the revulsion he feels
for his own body—I'm so ugly naked,
he confides. It frightens the women†.
The two sit on the terrace of the Hotel
Lutetia—about them, a dusty autumn
air varnished by the gasoline of endless
passing cars. I can't go to public baths
because I daren't walk down to the water.
He leans close, only to pull a white hair
       from the darkness of
her coat. He holds it before her eyes. *Je suis
une ruine féerique**, she admits in   *I am an enchanting ruin.
     a type of vanity.

† Oezle, Loy tells us, seems to be able to manage sex only with black
prostitutes—his "ebony wives" as he refers to them—and most often in pairs.

                    ***

Meanwhile, in Loy's apartment

¹⁹³⁴ Keep in touch with Breton,
Levy asks of Loy. But the Surrealist
is well-advanced in his own agenda—
that is, persuading Loy to let him publish what
survives of Cravan's manuscripts. It will be
a project, he feels, to be quickly achieved
by flattery, if not simply by his sheer

presence in her apartment. `In his eyes,`
he will say, Cravan's works `depict an atmos-`
`phere of unrefined genius à l'état brut.`
Breton, large-headed, and 'hairy at the heel',
as it's said*, arrives at her apartment
with `the expression of an outrageous ram`
in the company of his wife[†] (in Loy's eyes

> `a reanimated`

`mummy of an Egyptian sorceress).`
Still at the door, Breton comes to the point: `In`

> `my eyes,` he bows, he scrapes,

`your husband's works depict an atmosphere`
`of unrefined genius à l'état brut.`

> `My husband` [she replies], `would have been enraged at being`

`appropriated by the Surrealists, with their instability,`
> `and their woman-hating.`[††]

[†] Though the source does not name her, this is presumably Jacqueline Lamba
(Breton's wife from 1934 to 1943). Lamba studied at the *Ecole des Arts
Decoratifs* where she met, and became closely linked to, surrealist Dora Maar.

[††] Breton will make a second (and equally unsuccessful) attempt on the
Cravan manuscripts whilst in New York organising the *Surrealists in
Exile* exhibiton at the *Levy Gallery* in 1941. However, the following year,
Loy relents; she allows Cravan's notes to appear in *VVV*—one of the few
remaining journals devoted to the continued dissemination of Surrealism—
on the proviso that they are 'properly introduced'. In the Introduction, Breton
speaks of the work as embodying `an atmosphere of unrefined genius`
`à l'état brut.`

Oelze, Resumed

Shortly after the failure of their relationship [1936],
Oelze leaves by train (from the nearby station) to
Switzerland. A matter of hours after his departure,
Mina returns home, to find in her *salon* (still obstacled
with unsold lamps), a crowd of some twenty people,
gathered together at the end of the room. Six of these
are women, most of whom wear furs. The majority, the
men, are dressed in overcoats and hats (mainly fedoras).
Their backs are turned (though one man is facing the
room; another, an almost faceless profile). Nearly all of
the group are staring upwards, out through the opened
portes-fenêtres, across treetops toward a threatening
sky whose darkness could be impending night, or else
a gathering storm, or air at the brink of transforming
into flesh. An apocalypse is not beyond consideration.

Mina describes the gathering as `a tableau of unarrival`. Their unrevealed faces haunt her. `Whenever I'm in the room with those who wait`, she writes, `I catch myself looking at that sky — waiting for something to appear`.

Envoi

In 1936, with the continued rise of Hitler, Loy sells her apartment and leaves Paris for New York `whilst such a possibility remains`.

✱✱✱

New York

[1936] A year on from her
departure from Paris, Fabi[†] is un-
recognisable. Dressed in black she unites
`all the current types of beauty`, this exquis-
ite *mongrel* child of Cravan. Julien Levy
has continued to act as New York agent
for Mina's novel, *Colossus*—that 'un-
finished masterpiece' which (in Julien's eyes)
she used as a way to get money out
of him—touting it from publisher to
publisher without succcess.
His drinking
has become a problem; as have his affairs
with women from *the world of art*—shaking
his marriage to pieces.

[†] Fearing an invasion of France, Mina has sent her youngest
child to live with Levy and Joella in New York.

✱✱✱

And what of Mina
this once `exemplary woman`, coming
to New York a second time—reclusive,
inscrutable? In Joella's eyes at
her maddest. Surely she will **gas herself**,
as had Elsa von Freytag-Loringhoven [15 Dec., 1927];
or **shoot herself** like Jacques Rigaut [6 Dec., 1929] (though prob-
ably not employing a ruler to ensure

the bullet would pass through the heart); or Harry
Crosby [four days later] who **shoots himself** (two hours after
shooting his twenty-year-old lover [Josephine Rotch]); or Jules
Pascin [5 June, 1930] who **slits his wrists**[†]; or, most recently,
René Crevel [18 June, 1935] who **gasses himself**.

By way
of remedy, Joella arranges
         parties, sends a flurry—
une rafale, une véritable vague—of
invitations to her mother's friends from
         Paris and New York.
Mina, as is now her custom, locks herself
away in her room. That time of endless
         soirées, the world of
salons and cafés, mean nothing to her now.
These people are all strangers, amongst whom
     she chooses not to stand.

[†] Silence bleeding from his slashed wrists as Mina herself will express it in
her poem "Jules Pascin".

***

The Box-Maker, The Film-maker, *Mongrel*, and the Scientist

Between them, Boxmaker
and Madwoman, a great *affinity*. For him,
years before they meet, comes his entrancement
by the singular blue to be found in
the backgrounds of her paintings.[†]

And there she was:
author of that blueness, more than an ocean
away, trawling the flea-markets of Clignan-
court, selecting objects for his boxes—
watch-workings, twines, corks and tiny bottles,
marbles, thimbles, shells, and divers [19th Century] illus-
trations: from the digestive system to charts
of the moon. Not far behind her comes Levy,
on one of his frequent trips to Paris,
filming her searches[††]. Too much footage, of course,
         of her downturned head,
too much of her soft mouth; of the black hair
as yet un-loosened...

And then that other
    (one might think surprising)
commonality, which all three of them shared—
Mary Baker Eddy and her book on
    Christ, the scientist.

[†] Paintings exhibited at *Julien Levy Gallery* (Jan 28-Feb 18, 1933) her first
solo show in the United States, at which Cornell was present.

[††] Levy will go on make a short Surrealist film "full of exquisite portraits, full
of motion", of Mina Loy in the business of shopping at the flea markets.

***

Cornell

ONE OF MANY SUCH CONVERSATIONS
(MINA'S APARTMENT)

*Je pensais de même que notre jeunesse
était fini et le bonheur manqué.*

Alain-Fournier (1886–1914)

He shakes his head, No, he hasn't heard of Alain-
Fournier, nor his novel, *Le Grand Meaulnes.*

It's the summer of 1943 and Mina has invited
Joseph Cornell, artist and Christian Scientist, to lunch
at her apartment. He arrives, by bicycle, with a canvas
bag upon his back. Half an hour into their conversation
he rises and slides from the bag a narrow, glass-fronted,
oblong, wooden box (c. $11^{1/2} \times 15 \times 4$ inches), which he
carries to Mina, placing it in her waiting, outstretched,
hands. The work is heavier than she had expected.
It's a recent piece, he says. 'Setting for a Fairy
Tale'.

Behind the glass is a Photostat copy of an
engraving depicting a French château[†]. In its forecourt
are a number of tiny figures (various workmen,
guards, soldiers, dancing ladies in ball-gowns, and a
merchant, mounted on a horse: the players, perhaps,
in an unknowable drama?) Behind the château can be
seen snow-covered treetops—here, made from twigs
spattered with white paint. Beyond, is a dark winter's
sky.

Mina holds the theatrical view in her hands. She
notices that the windows in the Photostat have been

carefully removed from the original image, and instinctively brings the work closer to look inside their emptiness. What she sees is a partial image of her own face—the château has been glued to a mirror.

Cornell shakes his head. No, he replies.

It tells the story of Augustin Meaulnes, Mina explains, a young man who squanders the last of his youth in pursuit of the unobtainable Yvonne de Galais, whom he glimpses at a wedding feast held in a forsaken château[††]. It's also about the narrator — the fifteen-year-old François Seurel — as he becomes increasingly caught up in the older boy's quest. And she meets Cornell's eyes.

As you've probably guessed, Mina continues, there was a real Yvonne. And, having registered the box-maker's entrancement, she settles into the telling of Alain-Fournier's life. I should've begun 'once upon a time', she says — it's that sort of a story.

[†] In the Photostat, two corner wings have been scissored from the original engraving. Cornell will use the full château image in later works: in *Untitled (Rose Castle)*, 1945; *Le Chant du Rossignol* (c.1946-48); and *Untitled (Pink Palace)* c.1946-48. *Setting for a Fairy Tale*, will be the first in a series of thirteen *Palace* boxes he will make between 1942 and 1951.

[††] The château in Alain-Fournier's novel is most likely based on the château de Loroy, hidden in the Forêt de St-Palais, in Mery-ès-Bois.

THE BIOGRAPHY

Une fois [1905], whilst leaving an exhibition (the Fifteenth Salon of the Société Nationale des Beaux-Arts) at the Grand Palais de Paris, the eighteen-year-old Henri Fournier catches sight of a young woman walking arm-in-arm with an older lady—her mother, it transpires—and is sufficiently moved (that is, he has instantly fallen in love with the young woman) to follow them across the Seine to a house in the boulevard Saint-Germain. Over the next five days, he will return to this house at every opportunity waiting for the young woman to appear, but never knocking and introducing himself. On Sunday June 17, Whit Sunday, Henri, arriving for his vigil, finds her already on the boulevard, heading from the *5*[e] to the *6*[e] *arrondissement*—I am assuming you know the general arrangement of Paris[†]—where she will attend Mass at the church of Saint-Germain-des-Prés. The service taken, he follows her back out onto the street and, with admirable bravery, asks if he may walk with her. She agrees and they stroll to the banks of the Seine. He tells her he is a writer (or will be one day soon). She tells him her name is Yvonne de Quiévrecourt, and that she is staying in the city with relatives... but unfortunately she is leaving the next day. She takes her leave with the words *Nous sommes des enfants. Nous avons fait une folie.* We are children. We have behaved foolishly.

His own foolishness, however, continues. On the anniversary of his first glimpse of Yvonne, he is waiting at the steps of the Grand Palais in the naïve expectation of her reappearance; and, on several occasions, he returns to the boulevard Saint-Germain, in hope of seeing her once more at a window.

When finally he summons the courage to call at the house, he is told by the concierge that Yvonne had been married the previous winter. Sometime later, he hires a private investigator, from whom he learns her current address, and that she now has a child.

Eight years after first seeing her on the steps of the Grand Palais, he writes in a letter to Jacques Rivière editor of *La Nouvelle Revue Française* (which Mina dramatically paraphrases): Yesterday was the eighth anniversary of my seeing Yvonne Quiévrecourt. It's terrible to admit that even now I haven't lost hope. I can't believe God would have shown me so much and promised me so much and ended up giving me nothing.

And after this? Cornell is asking.

All I know, she replies, breathless still, from her recent impersonation, is that he joined the Army one month after the war began. And that he died fighting in Vaux-lès-Palameix one month later[††]. The story of Alain-Fournier's life, will diminish Cornell. Long after Mina Loy's departure late that afternoon, the box-maker continues to weep for the loss of Yvonne de Quiévrecourt. For many months, he finds it impossible to rid himself of the idea that *he* was the one who pursued—and was still pursuing, pointlessly—this young woman.

---

† Cornell had never been to Paris. As Leila Hadley noted in an interview (1971), 'He had only been to Nyack [NY] and that was it'—which is not strictly true, as he had been to Andover, Mass. as a child; but he had never travelled beyond New England.

†† Fournier joined the French army as a lieutenant in August, 1914. He was killed in action in a wood of firs, close to the village of Saint-Remy-La-Colonne (Meuse), on 22 September, 1914. Death resulted from a single bullet which passed through his sternum and second right rib. His body was discovered in a group grave in 1991, and was buried with full military honours in the cemetery of Saint-Remy-la-Calonne. The endplay of Fournier's relationship with Yvonne de Quiévrecourt is considerably complicated and the details would not have been known to Mina Loy. See Robert Gibson's *The End of Youth*, Exeter, 2005.

ONE OF MANY SUCH CONVERSATIONS
(CORNELL'S BASEMENT)

1944 Early the following year, 'returning the call', Mina visits Cornell at his mother's house in Utopia Parkway [No. 3708], Flushing, Queens. The previous night there had been a heavy snowfall and her first sight of the house presented itself as a painting which (were it not for the windows' dark oblongs and the central brick chimney), might evoke a study in white-on-white: requiring its observer to deduce a shape from elementary principles of engineering†.

Cornell (who has been keeping a look out) meets Mina at the glass-enclosed front porch, showing her into the living room—for years now the domain of Robert.††

It's such an extravagant name, she says, 'Utopia Parkway'. But then, I imagine, everyone must say that?

He leads her down to the basement of the house—*his* domain; the place he uses as a workshop. Not too many drop by here to warrant the term 'everyone', he says, then answers the issue of extravagance. Back in 1905, he starts, a group of investors calling themselves the UTOPIA LAND COMPANY bought fifty acres near Flushing. He pauses mid-flight. They wanted to set up a Jewish colony — a second Lower East Side. Never happened. The only trace of it is the name, seven-miles-worth.

And they resume their descent to the studio.

One wall is entirely made up of shelves given over to cartons filled with general bric-à-brac, children's toys, and late nineteenth century paraphernalia of every description. Cartons are labelled by their generic contents—DOLLS, DRIFTWOOD, LOVE LETTERS, MARBLES, MIRRORS, PEGS, PHOTOS, SEA SHELLS, SEQUINS, STAMPS, STUFFED BIRDS, TINFOIL, TINY TAPS AND TWIGS ^{Not, though, in alphabetical order}.

From another shelved wall he eases out a selection of completed boxes (stored upright, like folio books), their internal spaces sub-divided into compartments. Most have a clear glass cover. The juxtapositions of objects are, by turns, startling or intuitively instructive. Mina stares into their worlds. `Such reticent, such riotous, art`, she whispers. As for the frames, she learns how Cornell ages them to an appropriate antiqueness. Some he leaves out in the weather. Others are lightly cooked in the oven.

At this point, he is telling her about his recent work—a new series of enchanted châteaux, derived (he's delighted to tell her) from *Le Grand Meaulnes* which, since he last saw her, he has read ^{in the translation by Françoise Delisle, entitled *The Wanderer*, 1928} and re-read.

From above, *her* domain, comes the hectic pacing (back and forth, back and forth) of his mother, about her cleaning chores. The run of water in the pipes reaches them. As does the subsequent plate-clatter, and some sharp bickering from the cutlery.

`I found a copy of the Alain-Fournier in Schulte's... you know it, Schulte's? In lower Fourth Avenue — Bookseller's Row, they used to call it. You'd probably know Schulte's; how long have you been in New York?`

`Since 1936`, she answers. `But I was here before then. Two years, it would have been — 1916-17.`.

`Same time as Theo Schulte opened his Book Store`, Cornell notes. `Never much liked the tone of Schulte himself — but that was just the way he was, I suppose. Schulte's was one of the largest shops in the city. Very large basement. Very large main floor. It's got balconies, did you know that?`.

† Clement weather would have shown her *een Nederlands koloniaal huis*, wood-framed, two-and-a-half storeys high; one of four identical structures closely set, each on a quarter-acre unfenced lot.

†† Cornell's younger brother, Robert (b.1910)—to whom Joseph remained selflessly devoted throughout his life—suffered from cerebral palsy and was wheelchair-bound until his death in 1965.

Afterword

At the time of Loy's meetings with Cornell his life patterns have already been long drawn—his dedication to his younger brother, Robert; his obsessive and highly deferential relationship with his mother.

He will remain hopelessly attracted to film starlettes and young ballerinas†, many of whom will take 'centre stage' in his glass-topped wooden boxes.

Sustained by a powerful self-delusion, he will never relinquish his belief in childhood as a state of perfection— to admit otherwise would be to perish of despair.

He will continue to dwell in the same Utopia Parkway house till his death in 1972; outliving Mina Loy by some six years. His life will encompass no deep or long-lasting friendships—the closest probably being with the photographer Lee Miller, the painter Pavel Tchelitchew, and Marcel Duchamp. In his life there will be no requited love affairs. He will die a virgin.

† Film actresses include Rose Hobart, Greta Garbo, Hedy Lamarr, Lauren Bacall; ballerinas and dancers: Tamara Toumanova, Marie Taglioni and Renée "Zizi" Jeanmarie.

THE BOWERY POEMS

```
        so each of us must build from scratch
                       a ruin of ourselves.
```

They form a declension,
these addresses, their shift a trajectory.
From April [1944][†] Loy had stayed with Fabi through
the tail end of her marriage* at **302**   *to Hans Fraenkel
E. 66 Street. In [New Year] 1947 Mina is living in
a group house—run by "Klemp" (mother of Irene
Klempner, a friend of Fabi's)— at **36 E. 2nd
Street**, along with an acting student [Robert Lindsay] and the
mad Japanese woman with the scissors [Sakiko].
There are `frantic cats underfoot. The dishes`
`pile up and the grease collects. Fish heads lie`
`around the floor.` With evening, until deep
into darkness, from her window Mina
can see the red neon glow; feel its call.
      Six months later, they're
being evicted, the residents of 302,
moving *ensemble*, to a three storey house
    at **5 Stanton Street**.
[So it is] she passes through the `hell-vermilion`
`curtain of neon` to a street [and neighbourhood] the early
    Dutch named *bouwerij*.

[†] By this time, Julien and Joella will have divorced and remarried—he, to the
sculptor Muriel Streeter, a relationship also ending in divorce; and, in 1957, to
Jean Farley McLaughlin. Joella had only recently married Herbert Bayer, an
ex-Bauhaus Austrian artist. Julien will continue to battle with alcoholism and
depression.

***

What Julien Levy Wrote

> *Gorky—with the sadness*
> *of the world permanently upon him.*
>
> Dorothea Tanning

The night was one where wind-driven rain was slicking
the tar, right-parted, the bulk of it swept back in a style
not to be seen for many years. Levy describes himself,
`not driving as fast as the rain,` through the

darkness (always threatening, this tangential force) with the car reaching the top of CHICKEN HILL—along with the question as to where it came from, this name? An enquiry so adamant that the moment recreates itself on his account: a sharp bend at the hill's crest presenting a flock of fool chickens, half hop, half flap, clumsy across the road to get to that other side, gasping, beaks open, squawking as the carriage backhands a trail of slaughter through their witless ranks, to the downward slope where his own skid begins—the brain overcranking its passage as the back wheels sideslip and the car jolts to a temporary halt, this briefest of moments, before it turns, slowly (as if it were in bed) over on its left side. He writes all *this* about the chickens from the past and the rolling car. But as for the passenger—the artist Arshile Gorky—and *his neck*, only that when he next sees him, he looks like some barbaric warrior in the strange armour of his leather and steel neck brace. That's it for the neck, and no mention at all about the damage to his painting arm and hand. Nothing on how an injury like that might impact on an alcoholic artist recently deserted by his wife, Magouch, taking the children with her. Nothing on how within a month Gorky took his own life, thinking maybe the best result would have been *for him to die in the crash*, which would, at least, glorify his life, its promise... He *does* detail, though, how Gorky had gone through the empty house, seeking out his favourite spots and preparing an individually-made noose for each of them—no easy task with the neck and the arm and the hand being in the state they were; and notes how the artist had left it to the last moment to choose the location—a shed he favoured in bad weather, in which he would read or dream alone. This particular day the 'shed noose' was secured to a rafter on which he had chalked Good-bye, my 'loveds'.

Levy tells us how the bad weather continued through a perfunctory funeral service, after which Magouche, soaked more than any of the mourners, as though the rain had sought her out, insists the grave be filled, *now*, as she stands there at its precipice and, being filled, how she stamped it down, the broken earth, stamped it down. Levy is silent on the decline of his own business, which had grown out of touch with the latest movements in art. Not a word either on his abuse of alcohol, his guilt, and depression.

But the *not*-writing-it—the neck, the arm and hand, the shed, the rafter, the 'loveds'—haunts him. It spills into his life, such that the gallery becomes `distasteful`, fills him with `revulsion`. He continues for one more season, during which he places his artists with appropriate dealers and holds a Gorky retrospective (November 16—December 4, 1948).

In the 1970s, Levy will set about compiling his memoirs, gathering the gallery archives around him, including invitations, brochures, reviews, and other related ephemera. He will work in a small writing studio on his Connecticut property.

It is unclear how the fire began.

***

Summer

1

   During the days she walks
this ^{bouwerij} neighbourhood, these ^{bouwerij} streets, as if once more
seeking Christ the Scientist. Perhaps so.
At first light, find her circling the *cul de sacs*
of vacant lots, trailing unswept gutters, as
down-headed and focussed as she'd ever been
at Clignancourt, eyes only for *resources*
she might add to the refuse that accum-
ulates in her second floor room. By mid-
morning she is joined by the `hueless` strangers
that mooch these streets, their bodies draped in the
`eerie undress` of `mummies half-unwound`;
none aware of the shearing blades, or the click
of the finger rings, *behind* them (oblivious
      to the motion of his
unseen hand): Time's lank `contortive` tailor—
the cutter—choosing which of them to render
   `irreparable`.

2

In the streets of this **place**
of tramps, there are mostly ends of things: shoe heels,
can lids; tickets stubs*; a book of matches   *movie, bus.
sans heads; a crushed picture of a camel...
that is, parts that have come loose, been torn away.
She gathers them for a project not yet clear
in her mind, returning, through `the sedative`
`descent of dusk`—the air abrased electric.
From beyond the tenements comes the distant
unnamed war of soundless summer lightning.
It is growing dark. Now the heat shifts to
conflagrations of blinking red neons[†].
The landings of fire-escapes already
    filled with sleeping children.

[†] Over time she will tease out the [mongrel] shades of reds—from the French:
coquelicot, ponceau, vermeillon; the German: *stammel*; and Italian: *solferino*...

Winter

Sometimes, early as Oct.,
those grown weary of survival or simply
having fallen (accidentally*) in an open   *per ongeluk
place, freeze to death; their [anonymous] bodies carried off
at early light by a **ravenous** truck
more usually collecting [as Loy will put it] `a refuse`
`more profuse than man.`
                        At nine, the first wave of
the living emerge from the sardine-tin lines
of a wayside chapel's pews. Pulling others
after them [or so it appears], from the lee of a porch-stoop
or a shop's verandah. By now, she knows
everyone of them by face and *neke-name*;
as they know her as *the duchess** (seeing her   *de hertogin
as 'one of ours').
                Mid-day gone, the *residue*,
    `embalmed` (already!)
by rum, stagger through a pale-sunned daylight:
`inferno-faced, limbs sailing, flailing in`
        `disequilibrium.`

By late-afternoon the `Communal Cots`*
appear in side-streets and in cul-de-sacs;
      at the pale-light's first
failing, a pool of nine, ten, derelicts,
swaddled in rags, *sleep*, curled `grub-like` on the
      flagstones—those fallen
by exhaustion or by forsakenness [Stations 3 and 7]; those
for whom falling is no impediment
      to their salvation.[‡]
At the gathering's edge, outside the `Cot`'s near-
silence, near-stillness: `a derelict` in
      trembling delirium,
stretched out, face down (a voice sounding from a
passer-by: `Well, will you look at that man`
   `lovin' up the pavement!`)

* 'And always on the trodden street/—the communal cot...' *from* "Hot Cross Bum".

[‡] `In this broken world,` she will write to Mabel Dodge, `holiness is necessarily a broken thing – was not Christ's broken body the way to salvation.`

Aside

From Joella comes news [April,1949] that Levy has closed his gallery. That he had never shed the guilt of Gorky's death.

Three Collages

Communal Cot
Collage of cardboard, paper and rags
(c.1949?)

    Not the vertical planes
of easel and gallery wall, but from observ-
ation caught in *down-sight* (as at Clignancourt);
so that to her, pendant in low-air, they appear
as if by some extraordinary mastic-
ation, to have fallen full-grown, from the mouth
of God; papier mâché cocoons, in a mongrel-
mix of vagabond and angel—these `bandaged`
`thins`, their forms, curled or elongated; holy
speech made visible. Ten, she counts, within
this cot ^{this box, this ring, this stage}, *the outcast*[†] for a time of ruin:
brood of sleeping newborn; safe within their
swaddling bands, at the point of rising from
    flagstones of cardboard.

[†] A dramatis personæ?

No Parking
Mixed Media Collage
(c.1951)

    His face seraphic.
Floating man in his state of bliss, ^{it would seem} uplifted
by a backlane trash can, on whose opened lid
rests a butterfly* ^{from Veracruz}—its wings of flattened   *una mariposa
paper cup; its body the metal spiral
of a can-top. His companion[†] sleeps at
the bin's base, wrapped in a gown ^{a Rossetti Saint?} that adheres to[††]
a body ^{in strange curvature} managing to embrace itself.
The foreground is filled with spilled rubbish
including ^{bizarrely enough} a blackened banana skin.
Two bodies then—on which decay gathers
with the ease of autumn leaves tumbled to
some corner place—in their dreamings and contem-
    plations of th'eternal.

[†] Biographers and critics refer to this lower figure's gender as male; yet a
closer examination presents the profile of a (young) woman, or, at least, an
androgyne.

[††] That is, as if the body were `pressed` with `sweat-sculptured cloth`.
See Loy's "On Third Avenue".

Christ on a Clothesline
Kristus på en klädstreck
Collage and mixed media in deep
glass-covered box
(c.1953)

    As she has, several
times before (paying in cash), she uses
the fisherman as her model: the emac-
iated Scandinavian*. This time he is   *Swen
Christ, linen-thin, with yellow-khaki flesh,
pegged by his shoulders to the clothesline on
a tenement roof. His hands hang palm-up,
imploring the help of the viewer who
moves quickly on. The expression of the Christ-
face could be witnessed any day amongst
the beggars of the *Bouwerij*—that is, the regard
of those inexplicably forsaken;
unaware (as is their kind) *they shall ascend**,   *de ska stiga upp
    their flock glimmering.

The Last of the Bowery

¹⁹⁵³ The lease on N° 5
is running out. And with it, the family,
grown into needs for separate lives, breaks apart.
Alex Blossom* finds a room for Loy across   *of AL's BAR, *Bouwerij*
the street at N^o18*. The sum of her   *And one at N^o16 for Klemp.
resources—torn-offs and off-scourings, leavings,
discards, and, more recently, *perishables*—
are moved piece-by-piece, hand-to-hand (as might
be *reliques*) over Stanton by a chain of
angel derelicts.
              But no sooner, it seems,
than Mina has settled, Fabi is at
her door: `You must come to Aspen`*, she is, breath-   * Colorado, pop. 900.
lessly, saying. `There's a room fallen vacant`
`just across the hall from us. Fritz`[†]`has paid`
  `three months in advance`
      `to secure it for you.`^{††}
                  Perhaps it's the
altitude, Loy writes Cornell, `but as soon as`
    `I arrived, my hair`
`literally stood on end, and crackled`
`with electricity. Needless to say,`
  `I am not at ease here.`

[†] Fritz Benedict, an architect strongly influenced by Frank Lloyd Wright,
married Fabi in 1949. Theirs was a union largely match-made by Joella and
Herbert Bayer after Fabi's separation from Hans Fraenkel in 1948. Through
his collaboration with Paepcke and Bayer, Benedict became the foremost
architect in Aspen, and helped establish the town's signature style of modern
architecture.

^{††} Mina will travel by train to Aspen and move into the room "which is just
waiting for her", across the hall from her daughter and son-in-law. When the
Benedicts—with Mina in tow—move to their new house on Red Mountain,
she finds herself depressed by its isolation. Fortuitously, an apartment
becomes available in the building where Loy had originally stayed and she
moves back. This new accommodation is much bigger than she had before,
giving her a bed-sitting room and a light-filled front room which can be used
as a studio.

Aspen

In Aspen, people
still ride their horses into town. In Aspen
there is one paved street; the remainder, broken
asphalt or, more commonly, dirt. Here, **trodden**,
is not an adjective for streets[†]. In Aspen,
there are no *clochards*—she grieves the loss of
the Cots and their fallen. Grieves the fire escapes
with their summer nights' ragbag of slumbering
children. A trolley's [transient] brilliancy in the dust.
An unknown dawn strewn with prophecy.
In Aspen, Joella still rents the room
at 18 Stanton Street lest Mina decide
to return. And everywhere there's talk of
    The Aspen Idea.[††]

[†] More commonly, one picks a path. One criss-crosses. Steps over. Everywhere,
one's feet are placed with circumspection.

[††] That is, industrialist Walter Paepcke's re-imagining of Aspen as an
international resort destination and centre of a cultural florescence, promising
**great books, great men, great music... Forget what you think
you know about our mountain town; come and experience "The
Aspen Idea" for yourself.** The husbands of Joella and Fabi played key
roles in Paepcke's vision, as, on a lesser scale, did Joella and Fabi themselves—
famously including their refurbishment of the *Hotel Jerome* and the
organisation of large-scale projects for the *Institute of Humanistic Studies.*

    Prior to The Aspen Idea, Paepcke—the largest landowner in Aspen—
had been a mass producer of cardboard containers; the connection of
cardboard and Loy, here, is irresistible.

✱✱✱

Mina doesn't return
to the Bowery. But her collages remain
hung in Stanton Street—her room become an
ersatz gallery for visiting dealers
and artists. When Joseph Cornell visits,
the power of what he sees **jolts him back outside
to catch his breath**[†]. When Duchamp pays his respects
with gallery owner David Mann*, the works   *Owner of the Bodley Gallery.
convince them to mount a show at Bodley* (it's   *Opening 14th April, 1959.
decided 'then & there'), called **Mina Loy's
'Constructions'**.[††]

            She holds the invitation now.
Esther's about the cleaning part of her day[†††].
She can hear the irrhythmic tap of broom-
    head against skirting board.

† Roger Conover gives: Cornell was reportedly so moved by what he saw that he "had to step into the kitchen to catch his breath". *TLLB* (Carcanet, 1985) p.*lxxviii*.

†† Technically, low-relief, three-dimensional constructions; Duchamp comments in the visitor's book: `Hauts-reliefs et bas-fonds, Inc. Marcel Duchamp (admiravit);` Julien Levy describes them as being `Whole in their fragmentation.`

††† With the Benedicts' and the Bayers' new business-demands drawing them increasingly out of town, Joella and Fabi sought out a companion for Mina. Their choice was a fifteen-year-old school girl called Esther Jane Herwick. Esther must wash dishes, sweep floors, and generally tidy the house without touching any of the what-looks-like-rubbish in Mina's studio. She must brush Mina's now curled and netted white hair, and be a patient listener to her (long) repeated tales. Meals must be prepared *without question*—especially exotic combinations such as ground raw liver and grapefruit juice.

✱✱✱

At the opening, Duchamp
poses for a Berenice Abbot photo-
graph alongside *Bums Praying*. His body
blocks most of the adjacent assemblage†,
though it is possible to see a figure,
angel or derelict (from the photo,
it's impossible to tell which) whose naked
foot already *hangs down beyond the frame*.
How simple it would be to slip away
from this cluttered universe.
                    With her health
deteriorating, Joella and Fabi
move their mother to a Victorian
double-storey guest house under the watchful but caring
    eye of Frau Bibbig.

† This adjacent piece has, suitably enough, been lost, as have a great number of Loy's works; the later constructions, in particular, rotting, disintegrating... not unlike a conversation that can only be recollected, not preserved.

✱✱✱

Chez Mrs Bibbig

AN EPILOGUE

The teeth inside my ears are making such a noise,
please excuse me, I don't know how
I manage to read at all.

Mina Loy

1

They arrive, this early
afternoon $^{\text{August 1965}}$, the two young men—the poet,
and the editor—Paul Blackburn, Robert
Vas Dias[†]. The tape, as they say, *rolling*,
picks up preliminaries, including
THE STORY OF HER ^{new} DENTURES, encompassing
A GENERAL HISTORY OF HER TEETH—an imped-
iment she still bemoans. **I never had
any teeth all my life** $^{\text{since her early teens}}$, she tells the young men.
And, as if by way of emphasis, shifts the plates
around her mouth, like clackedy-clackedy-
clack. Every day, before the mirror, she clacks
her false teeth around her mouth. The motion
        borders on the erotic.

[†] The full transcript of this interview can be found in: "Mina Loy Interview
with Paul Blackburn and Robert Vas Dias. (Introduction by Carolyn Burke.
Transcribed by Marisa Januzzi and Carolyn Burke)", in *Mina Loy: Woman
and Poet*, ed. Maeera Shreiber and Keith Tuma, Orono, Maine, The National
Poetry Foundation, 1998, pp. 205–243. Other than a brief outbreak of
laughter, Mrs Bibbig's contribution to the tape is the interjection: *Es ist immer
so. Ein Prophet ist in seinem Vaterland nie zu Hause.* [It's always like that. A
prophet's never at home in his fatherland].

✱✱✱

2

My second husband,
she is clarifying for them, **Cravan,**
was—how should she put it?—**perfectly solid**
everywhere.
        Mina Loy, coquette, has al-
ready seized the young men's attention. Even
now $^{\text{æt 82}}$ she has not forgotten the secrets
of charm, the benefits of flattery.

In their company she becomes, by her
own admission, `charmingly loquacious`.
On the ^{false} assumption that Mr Vas Dias
is Spanish, Mina has dressed `en moda`
`española`—is that right, she asks herself? [†]
Going on—`Caballero, permíteme`
   `bailar para usted`.[††]

[†] Spanish never being one of her happier languages.

[††] Something like, "Gentlemen, permit me to dance for you".

3

For the first time that afternoon the interviewers
notice a Flamenco guitarist seated in the corner of the
room.

The performance, Mina explains, will include
toque (guitar playing), *baile* (dance), *jaleo* (vocaliza-
tions), *palmas* (handclapping), *pitos* (finger snapping)
and *dentadura postiza*.

`The last term, 'dentadura postiza', could`
`be translated as 'dental castanets'`, she says, and
draws a pair of teeth from her mouth. `These days`
`I call them my 'castanets in the rhythm of a`
`danza de la muerte, 'a dance of death', as we`
`say here in Aspen. Let us hope they don't work`
`this afternoon.` [*Laughter*]

`Our guitarist for today,` she continues, `is`
`Pablo Apellido. Pablo is a local musician and a`
`frequent visitor to the house.`

As they will later admit in their respective
autobiographies, both men experience a rush of
jealousy.

With the dance finished, Mina retreats to a table
and lowers the dentures into *a bol à poisson*[†].

`You know they watch me,` she says. `If they've a`
`mind to, some days they'll keep it up for hours.`
`It's very disconcerting.`

`Have you thought of placing a dark cloth`
`over the glass?` Vas Dias, delicately, suggests.

`But that, signor, would be like throwing a`
`puppy out into the cold.`

[†] A fish bowl—in this instance filled only with water.

The recording continues with the two young men insisting that she read some of her poems—during which, they praise her words and her renditions highly. To her mind, the afternoon has been a splendid success. The teeth, however (in their own way, jealous of all three young men), remain an ever present distraction smiling at the poetess and her admirers from their vantage point in the fish bowl.

How difficult it must have been for her during 'the Paris years'—such a beautiful young woman, with her grey-blue eyes, her hair unloosed in its black cascade covering her thighs, drawing from her mouth an upper, then a lower plate.

As for the Aspen interview, it has moved on; and we have unfortunately missed that section of the conversation. Back in the present, Mina is reciting a selection of her poems, egged on by—at times, embarrassingly frequent—plaudits from the young men. Amongst these poems are "Lunar Bædeker", "Parturition", "Pig Cupid" (and other sections from "Love Songs"), "Jules Pascin", Part 2 of "On Third Avenue", "Stravinsky's Flute", and "Joyce's Ulysses"..

`That's a very good description of Joyce's prose`, Blackburn is remarking.

`Yes it is. Well, thank you.`

(tape ends here)*

THE VOLLARD SUITE

1

He has fallen asleep again, having a propensity for it,
the 'giant ape'; this huge, glooming, swarthy
man, whose forehead bulges like a serve of ox tongue.
It begins like this: [1895] with Vollard at twenty-nine kneeling
in the cramped under-counter of a Seine-side second-hand
book and print seller's stall, seeking
to decipher signatures by torchlight. Amongst the rolled
canvases he finds art by someone Pollock, someone
Hockney, someone Warhol, someone Bacon...
not one of them an artist whose work he has seen before.
How much for these? he asks from the darkness in a high-pitched,
lisping tone. *Twenty francs a piece, comes the reply.*
Thirty francs for the ones that use a lot of paint.
Forty for the Pollock.
                              His new gallery—on rue Lafitte,
              the centre of the art world
in Paris—is barely 10ft wide. It is here that
he plots his greatest coup. He will oversee the return
              of Cézanne from more than twenty
years of exile in Provence. A one-man show.
He knows the risk involved—Cézanne is known
              everywhere as a madman or an impostor.
Even the avant-garde hold him in contempt. Vollard says,
I bought one hundred and fifty canvases from
      him, almost his entire output.

2

Cézanne dies and the prices for his paintings soar.   1906
Vollard is set up for life. He purchases a Left
Bank mansion in rue Martignac [7e]. His Lafitte gallery
becomes a meeting point for a bohemian crowd of artists
and collectors. For thirty years, every Friday, except public
holidays, he holds Creole Chicken Curry Nights
(remembered from his Réunion recipés) in the bare-walled cellar.
As for his mansion, Brassai reports, there are only
two rooms one can inhabit—a dining room, a bedroom.
The rest of it given over to stored artworks, many
unframed, loosely piled. Nearly twenty thousand   1936

Vollard estimates—Cézannes, Renoirs, Picassos, Matisses,
Gauguins, Van Goghs, Degas, Cassatts, Monets,
Manets, (as well as a substantial group of works by
        painters who will not come into
prominence until the last half of the Twentieth
Century—some are still unborn) piled high, dust-ridden,
    unframed, in impressive disorder.

   3

For Ambroise Vollard it ends like this—chauffered   1939
to his mansion, probably asleep in the passenger seat
of his black Talbot convertible. In the deceptive accumulations
of an afternoon's fine rain, his car races along
the Route Verte, from his cottage in Le Tremblay-sur-Mauldre
to rue Martignac, Paris. Approaching the junction to Jouars-
Pontchartrain the Talbot planes across wet tar. Vollard,
awakened by the sudden shift of direction, catches
a white blur, a slash diagonalled between life
and death. And, like a huge mechanical black
athlete, the Talbot somersaults, twice in mid-air.
The world upends itself. The long nose of
the car—proportionally longer than an Afghan's snout—
sniffing out the roadside poplar-row hurtles
        itself towards those things which
are brutally still. Before him everything stops.
The dealer and his chauffeur remain anchored in space
        and time. All that is behind however
continues to rush forward. Objects arrive from the back ledge,
one of them fracturing Vollard's neck. Within
        a matter of seconds, everything
is reduced to stillness; if not silence. He outlives his chauffeur
by eight hours, held, excruciated on the rack
        of his own body. What remains
forever unsettled, is whether his was death by sculpture
(a Maillol brass[†]) or by the ironware pot used to cook
    Creole Chicken Curry.

[†]Aristide Joseph Bonaventure Maillol (1861–1944) began his career as a
painter, printmaker, and tapestry designer/weaver. Due to failing sight, from
1901 onwards he worked almost exclusively as a sculptor. Not unlike Vollard,
Maillol died in an automobile accident when, during a thunderstorm, the car
in which he was a passenger skidded from the road and rolled over.

Picasso
A Shorter Life

1 Smoke

1881 Don Salvador blows cigar smoke into the nostrils of his still-born nephew, making of him a living soul. Thus, a marvellous being comes into the world—a magus, with the moral inclinations of a corpse. Looking back at his life, everything seems to have happened swiftly—a tumble of betrayals, marriages; infidelities of every kind. Perhaps biography's unforgiving distillation lends to these liaisons the sense of lasting no more than a matter of months. Not so. These attachments are stretched over years. It is crucial here you understand the time scale. The distortions, the inherent cruelty of slowness.

2 Olga

1917 For a man with no interest in music outside of flamenco, who judges dancing as immoral and depraved, it might seem ill-considered to take a ballerina for a wife. Olga Khokhlova comes to Paris with Diaghilev's troupe: one of those dancers he likes to include from a higher social class. The newly-weds take rooms in rue La Boétie, amidst the antique shops and galleries. Pso dresses now from Savile Row, in double-breasted tweeds. He slides a gold watch from his pocket. Paints his wife as would a Realist. 'I want to recognise my face,' she insists in cow-accented French, intolerable as his own. She screams, drinks coffee. Both, it seems, obsessively. She bears him a child, Paulo, in whom Pso has no interest beyond the age of four. The artist describes his son as 'ordinary'—that most dismissive of character traits, at one stage employing him as his chauffeur. But he drinks. Dying at fifty-four from cirrhosis of the liver, a legacy of drug and alcohol abuse.

3 Marie-Thérèse

1927 Pso (as Andalusian flâneur, out this early afternoon, freeing himself of Olga's screech and clattering), saunters near the Metro OPÉRA to find, amongst 'the apparition of these faces' labouring upwards to a bitter January air, a seventeen-year-old girl, Greek-nosed, with eyes of blue-grey. He grabs her arm, pulls her from the flow. *I'm Picasso!* he announces, *We are going to do great things together.* Her name is Marie-Thérèse. She has never heard of Picasso; knows nothing of Modern Art, preferring BICYCLING, GYMNASTICS and MOUNTAINEERING. He takes her virginity at a children's camp in Dinard and, finding her sufficiently submissive, installs her in an apartment in rue La Boétie across the road from Olga. His sexual demands are bizarre. Some make her laugh at the thought of them—but he hates her laughter. He prefers to keep her tearful. 'Most of it was sadism,' Marie-Thérèse confirms. 'First rape, then work. Nearly always like that.'

4 Minotaur

1930 Ambroise Vollard, collector, art dealer, commissions from Picasso 100 etchings in the neoclassical style. Before too long the Minotaur appears. First, sharing a saucer of champagne with a bearded sculptor, then joining him in bed with his model. Six weeks later Marie-Thérèse tells Pˢᵒ she is pregnant. The artist is terrified. Is it possible that by the sheer force of his genius one of his creations has impregnated his current lover? Needless to say, the unthinkable comes to pass. A male child, covered with blood-red oils, is born to the young girl and the Spanish artist. Vollard feels in some way responsible for what has happened and mother and child are quickly secreted in his house in Le Tremblay-sur-Mauldre, ten miles from Versailles. For several months the creature remains hairless; what will be horns are barely knuckle-like lumps. The genitals, an inheritance from Picasso, are fully formed and would be of prodigious size even for an adult. From the first, Marie-Thérèse deems it satanic. She quickly learns how it shies away from candle-light, rears, swivelling aside with astonishing dexterity. Mercifully, the horned boy dies, *par hazard*, glimpsing its own grotesqueness in a glass—death by self-sight—a condition previously noted in creatures half-bull, half-human. Later, as a consequence, Marie-Thérèse always ensures a candle burns when Picasso demonstrates an urge for rutting. The candle is an addition which the artist finds exciting—this fragile token of romance to complement buggery.

5 Dora Maar

1936 Then there is the matter of the Jugoslavian photographer. Henriette Theodora Markovich. P^so is introduced to her by Éluard. He has seen her just a few days back at the café Deux-Magots. Seen her, black-haired, dark-eyed. Born in Tours, she tells him, the same year as his *Les Demoiselles d'Avignon*. He takes her hand. She is wearing long black gloves embroidered with roses. Stained dark, the lace, at the webbing. He has seen the gloves as well, on that earlier occasion, folded, laid aside. Away from her splayed hand pressed palm-down on the wooden table top. She had been playing a familiar Jugoslavian game. Stabbing rapidly with a knife between her fingers. Blood already flowing from a wound close to the second finger's knuckle. She seemed fascinated by the risk, the sudden pain. He recalls her now a sometime mistress of Bataille. P^so enquires as to whether she might present him with a gift of her gloves? That night, that week, sleeplessly, he dreams of her, at her forbidden games. He, peering out from beneath a table, sees her—spectacled, black-ribboned at her neck. Sees her in that bourgeois drawing room with its rugs and its striped wallpaper. Sees her riding on the back of Bataille. What mightn't she do. He falls abandonedly into imaginings—thrusting in the air, his penis wrapped in the silk of that black glove. P^so, priapic, rapacious, sees it all from where he sits cross-legged beneath the table. The little Andalusian boy.

6 Commission

1937 As part of a commission to create a mural-sized painting for the Spanish Pavilion at the *Exposition Internationale des Arts et Techniques*, Juan Larrea acquires an appropriately sized studio for Picasso's exclusive use: the giant top-floor attic of 7 rue des Grands-Augustins, where Balzac had written his 'The Unknown Masterpiece'. Its floor is paved with small red tile hexagons many of which have been broken in clusters beneath the weight of three centuries worth of ponderous furniture. There is a view (opening up the pair of twelve-paned windows) across geometrical hills of rooftops, chimney stacks; ridges of terraces skittled with chimney pots. Marie-Thérèse remains in Vollard's Tremblay-sur-Mauldre house. During the week P^{so} sleeps at his new studio, still within the range (it comes to him, a tinnitus) of Olga's screams. Meanwhile, a street away in rue Savoie, Dora waits to be summoned.

7 Painful

1937 In his paintings Marie-Thérèse grows fatter, uglier. One night he enters the bedroom to see her seated (half-turned back from the dressing table at his footfall) her face that of a victim of some monstrous stroke, her nose and forehead become one swollen, drooping, doughy, appendage. Over the following days the dismemberment begins—eyes, fingers, nipples, float on a white background. Now every part of her is obliterated. He draws close to his audience: 'It must be painful for a girl to see in a painting that she is on the way out.' Meanwhile, with little more than a month to go before the *exposition*, Picasso still has no subject for the Spanish Pavilion's empty forty metres.

8 Guernika (1937)

Out from the fields beyond Guernika, barely audible above the relentless bomb-bursts, the fire-roar and the collapse of masonry, comes the sound of mechanical ratatat against a hideous silence. The German aeroplanes are machine-gunning flocks of sheep.

9 The Effect of Fear

1937 Late May, with *Guernica* still a cartoon laid out in black and grey, P^so holds a luncheon at the Grands-Augustins studio. The table is set up, centred on the French doors. Seated before him are Giacometti, Ernst, Breton, Roland Penrose and Henry Moore. Late in the afternoon, over the plate of cheeses, P^so begins a monologue.

'The woman running from the little cabin on the right,' and he leans back in his chair, 'with one hand held in front of her. Let me tell you,' he says, rising, 'there is something missing there.'

He leaves the room, coming back with a roll of toilet paper which he sticks on the woman's hand.

'There,' he says, addressing the table, 'that leaves no doubt about the commonest effect of fear.' He laughs. And everyone laughs with him.

10 Balls

1937 There is a Dora Maar photograph of Picasso from the mid-summer days spent at Mougins. The artist is seated, legs apart. One can see his balls shifting quietly in the Mediterranean air, as might buoys in the slightest of swells. Clocking against each other. Barely held in check by his swimming costume.

11 A Game of Cards

1937 P^so fans open his hand: a king of hearts and four queens. He smiles. But the pleasure is short-lived. At their first sight of him, the Queens begin to weep. Now they sob. Soon it will be clearly heard by those around the table in the smoke-filled room. Now, their minuscule tears fall to the tabletop. He yells at his cards to be quiet. *You are ruining everything*, he bellows. But already it is too late—*Hey, Pablo*, comes the voice of one of the players. *You wouldn't have the Weeping Queens again, would you?* Over time it becomes a stock phrase with which to taunt him: Picasso's got the *Queens* today.

12 Nocturne: Night Fishing in Antibes

1939 Back from Amboise Vollard's funeral, P^so finds a new guest at his Antibes studio—Jacqueline Lamba, wife of Breton, and Dora's friend since Art School. The two women spend days together on the beach. Here they are, this August night, promenading, nearly at the quay's edge. Dora with a double-headed ice-cream in her right hand, a bicycle wheeled by her left. There is a grace to them. The grace and serenity of a slow dance (somewhere a blues trumpet is playing, its melody broken, breathless, as though its improviser lay flat upon his back—*le jazz horizontal*). The air is filled with flying insects. Above, a sky blotched with crushed yellowed starlight. Stars of the myopic. Stars as they might appear through the eyes of a weeping woman. Below the stone quay-side, men lean out from a small fishing boat spearing fish attracted by the yellowed acetylene light-flare which deceives them into thinking it a sudden summer's day. When real morning comes, gun emplacements are being set up along the beach.

13 Nude Dressing her Hair

1940 At last he is able to express it. Here, he has captured her, the *essence* of her. Here, as he enters to find Dora naked before the mirror dressing her hair. He paints her that very evening from this memory— snouted, loose-fleshed, splay-footed, massively arsed and thighed. As dog-faced as the skeletal Kasbek, his malnourished Afghan hound. Barely held within the room in which she squats. Her body disgusts him. The thick hair. The darkening moustache. The seepages. The monthly mess with its ammoniac after-stench. He can no longer take the *air* of her into his body. Cannot bear its stinking passage through his nose, the aftertaste of it in his mouth. But what can be done? There is nothing else to do. He beats her repeatedly, often leaving her unconscious on the floor.

14 Goldfish

1943 in Paris, witnesses a particularly bitter winter. Brassaï's goldfish freezes to death in its tank. The studio of Grands-Augustins ices over. The war plays havoc with his artists' supplies. He turns to making figures from cut or torn paper. Using the tip of his cigarette to burn out the features of the face. P^{so} is in love again. A young Art student, younger by forty years, has come to his attention. She reminds him of Rimbaud and he finds the comparison pleasing, a *frisson*, captured by her fine androgyny, this Françoise Gilot.

15 Clippings

1946. Meanwhile, Dora crumbles beneath the ghostweight of Marie-Thérèse. She sits in a darkened room, staring at the naked insides of her fingers, the webbing. The flesh is scarred. Hatched with fine lines. It is how her whole body feels. As though a blade had passed over her every extremity, too close, too close. A thousand cuts. *Fear love*, she sings, *fear love*. Like some modern Ophelia. *Close the window. Open the window. Let the mirror be empty.*

P^{so} has Dora committed. Gives his consent to a program of electric shocks. On 'medical grounds' Doctor Lacan encourages her to convert to Catholicism. P^{so} moves about his audience, noting how he had never been in love with Dora Maar. 'I liked her as though she were a man. I used to say: "You don't attract me, you never have". Well, you can imagine the tears and hysterical scenes that followed!'

As for Marie-Thérèse, she will retain all his letters and, in tiny packages of tissue paper, his finger-nail clippings. It will take her another forty years before she hangs herself.

16 The Last of Dora Maar

1947 She packs two suitcases—one filled largely with grey clothes; the other, various painting materials. She takes a taxi to Gare de Lyon and a train to Avignon, where she is met and driven to a ruined house in the village of Ménerbes. So it is she moves between the Parisian winters and the summers of the Luberon. It is the life of a recluse, her body slowly curving down upon itself like a figure from her photomontages. In 1994 she falls. Dora is bedridden. The shutters of rue Savoie now remain permanently closed. She has a saucepan on which she beats two spoons to call Rosa. She constructs a series of strings with which she can pull necessary objects closer. She will only read books written in, or translated into, English. Three years later she dies alone in her apartment, beneath a large boxwood crucifix and surrounded by the stations of the cross. She has outlived Picasso by twenty-four years. *I am blind*, she writes. *Made from a clutch of earth. But your gaze never leaves me. And your angel keeps me. The soul that still yesterday wept is quiet.* Blood shakes its wings and alights from between the fingers of a glove. *This day*, she whispers, *was a sapphire. Here it is.*

17 Broomstick

1947 Françoise Gilot bears him a child. As usual, it makes him feel young again. He over-flows with energy. And then he feels the need to free himself.

'Look at you,' he derides. 'With all your ribs sticking out to be counted. Any other woman would improve after the birth of a baby, but not you. You look like a broom. Do you think brooms appeal to anybody? They don't to me.'

You will recall how, during the war, Picasso would fashion human figures from torn paper, burning in their features with a cigarette end. Here, now, with war a distancing memory, he returns to this technique. This time we encounter the little man with the dead eyes holding a cigarette to Françoise's cheek. It pits the skin, puckering the flesh around it, a tiny volcano smouldering on his so-called lover's face.

18 Thinking of Herself

1952 A Spring exhibition of Gilot's paintings is opened at Kahnweiler's. One which garners too much praise—a circumstance intolerable to *le maître*. P^so visits the major dealers. Her contract with Kahnweiler is terminated. Everywhere she turns, dealers tell her they cannot show any of her paintings—to do so would be to risk Picasso's displeasure.

Unlike her predecessors, however, she does not consider him a god. By the end of the year Françoise is confiding: 'I despise him. I can't forgive him for turning the person I loved into one I despise. He's become a dirty old man. It is all so grotesque and so ridiculous that I can't even be jealous.'

She informs P^so that she is going to marry the painter Luc Simon. 'It's monstrous,' he exclaims at the announcement, turning to the audience. 'She thinks only of herself! I'd rather see a woman die, any day, than see her happy with someone else.'

19 A New Afghan

1953 He is seated on a couch. He wears a t-shirt, loose shorts and square-toed sandals. His hands are clasped about his left knee. His legs have lolled apart, sufficient to provide a view (one dare only look for a second) of his famous sack and the monstrous balls that plot within. How he aches to show them to every woman, this bull's endowment. He shows them to his new Afghan, Kabul.

'But I do not have a woman,' he repeats over and over to the long snouted, doe-eyed, creature which seems to embody his misery.

'I am *wounded* without a woman.'

20 Jacqueline

1955 Then suddenly, his wounds are healed. At the Madoura Pottery in Vallauris where he fashions his ceramics, he re-acquaints himself with Jacqueline Roque, a young woman forty-five years his junior. Under her influence he begins a series of canvases and lithographs—variations on the theme of Delacroix's *The Women of Algiers*. The harem women all based on versions of Jacqueline. One February day, three days away from completing the series, he is taken by a sudden silence. The air clears a moment. As if wiped clean. A *coup de torchon*. What is it, this ceasing? It comes to him—a near-constant screaming has fallen away. It is no surprise that late in the afternoon he receives news of Olga's death.

21 Clothes

1957 He's kept them all, for years, these stick-figure's clothes, Françoise's dresses. Clothes belonging to a broomstick. Has kept them in a cupboard under lock and key. How he had come to hate them. And the body they had fitted so perfectly. But now he discerns a use for them—as he had often thought he might—that is, their utter inappropriateness for his new mistress.

'You don't need money for clothes,' he says. 'You need to choose something from the wardrobe.' And he leads her upstairs. Jacqueline can't fit into them. He goes through the mockery of making it possible. Lettings out. Constructing longer hooks. All of which serves to underline her own body's failings. The fabric tears.

22 Cobblestones

1962 It is said, in his years with Jacqueline, Picasso produced more works of art than with any other woman. In 1962, for instance, he paints her portrait 72 times; in 1963 he paints her portrait 160 times. But he grows old. He has already swapped his gaping shorts for long flannels, loosely cut. Two years later he undergoes surgery on his prostate. The long held belief that should he cease to work he would die, presses down increasingly upon him. *I paint*, he says, *just as I breathe*. He loses height at an alarming rate. Exhausted, terrified, barely over five feet tall, he works. In Spring of 1968 he begins a suite of what will be 347 etchings—brothel scenes, copulations, observed by various voyeurs, a dwarf, a clown, a jester, a king. A little Andalusian boy. How he has come to loathe his wife! What possessed him to *marry* her! He portrays her as *The Pissing Woman*—the hot yellow water hissing through her flaps, splashing back from the gutter against her thighs. For *her* part, Jacqueline is familiar with Picasso's own timid performances above the porcelain. The draining-off. The pitiful after-shake. The too-too dark colour of his offering. Nearby, streets are barricaded with overturned cars. Students are pulling up ancient cobbles for ammunition.

THE PAINTERS PORBUS AND POUSSIN
VISIT LE MAÎTRE AT HIS STUDIO IN RUE
DES GRANDS-AUGUSTINS 1973

Porbus and Poussin follow the twine along the near-lightless corridor and up a set of stairs, halting at the open doorway of the third floor studio. The space appears empty but for a cluttered workbench and, close by, a painting propped on an easel. Full of curiosity, the two men make their way to the canvas.

'Look at her', comes an exhorting voice. They turn towards its source. What they see, hunched in the corner of the room, surrounded by the fine bones of dead women (chained, broken, women) is an old leathery man, trembling in the half-darkness. A half-erection has grown from his forehead. He clutches a roll of toilet paper in his hand.

'Look at her!' the voice comes again. The two young men return their gaze to the canvas. They can, however, see nothing but a chaos of paint, criss-crossed by heavy dark lines. Porbus, moving closer to the canvas, eventually makes out the tip of a bare foot emerging from the visual disorder; its presence striking him, if anything, with the jolt of an oversight, a flaw of technique. Poussin admits he sees nothing but a squandering of paint.

'Nothing on my canvas!' comes the old man, raising himself from the floor; looking in turn at the painters and at his picture. 'Are you saying I'm a dotard. A lunatic! That I have neither talent nor power! That I am only a rich man, who works for his own pleasure, and makes no progress! You are jealous—that's what it is! You would have me think that my picture is a failure because you want to steal her from me! I can see her, I can see her,' he cries, 'and she is beautiful... a work of genius!'

***

23 Signing

1973 P^{so} clutches a swathe of lithographs to his woolly (pizzle-yellow) chest. 'I can't die now,' he trembles. (Has he wet himself?) '*Now* I must sign my works.' He picks up a coloured pencil. Separates the first of the prints, smooths it out. Scrawls in the corner: *Picasso.* Adds: *Greater than Matisse.* 'What day are we?' he calls to Jacqueline. 'Le 7 Avril.' 'And the year?' '1973.' 'Of course it is,' comes his reply. He adds the date. Draws forth another print: *Picasso. Greater than Manet*, 7.iv. MCMLXXIII. Takes another: *Greater than Velázquez*, 7.iv. MCMLXXIII...

24 Smoke

1973 Next day his heart specialist, Pierre Bernal, arrives; two hours before the artist's death. Never a tall man, recent years have shrunk Picasso to a near homuncular state. A brown wrinkled manikin drowsy in his cot. From the bed he tries to affect a joking manner. But his breath often fails him, and most of what he says cannot be understood. Only after the specialist has gone, does the engrossing begin. The skin, too sparse for the unexpected bloat within, tears apart at what looks to be points of old stitching, as though the *grand-maître* were a monstrous doll from one of Hoffman's tales. Jacqueline waits at the bedside, drifting in and out of momentary sleeps. She is, though, wide awake when death occurs. Don Salvador's cigar smoke is finally expelled through Picasso's nostrils drifting upwards, back into the still-breathing world. Jacqueline does not leave the bedside. Even when the corpse begins to rot. All of this, with over thirteen years to wait before she shoots herself.

NOTES

Rimbaud first appeared online in *Recent Australian Fiction* (*RAF*) Vol. 23, No.2, 2017. Sampling from Rimbaud was largely based around Oliver Bernard's prose translations in his *Rimbaud, Collected Poems* (Penguin, 1962), augmented by Louise Varèse's *Rimbaud: Illuminations and Other Prose Poems* (New Directions, 1957). Central biographical texts were Graham Robb's *Rimbaud* (Picador, 2000); Jean-Luc Steinmetz's *Arthur Rimbaud: Presence of an Enigma* (Welcome Rain, 2001); and Pierre Michon's wonderful *Rimbaud the Son* (Yale University Press, 2003). For the 'second half' of Rimbaud's life, the key text was Charles Nicholl's *Somebody Else: Arthur Rimbaud in Africa 1880-91* (Jonathan Cape, 1997), assisted by Alain Borer's *Rimbaud in Abyssinia* (William Morrow, 1984). Charles Cros' English Sonnets were assembled from mistranslations of the French originals. One of Cros' early poems (1872), "Le Hareng Saur", remains a popular poem with French children to this day, and was translated and illustrated by Edward Gorey under the title of "The Salt Herring".

Virginia Stephen is the first part of a projected longer work, "Woolf: A Shorter Life". Major primary sources for this early period were *The Letters of Virginia Woolf Volume I: 1888-1912 (Virginia Stephen)*, ed. Nigel Nicolson and Joanne Trautmann (Harcourt Brace Jovanovich, 1975); *Virginia Woolf: A Passionate Apprentice: The Early Journals 1897-1909*, ed. Mitchell A. Leaska (Harcourt Brace Jovanovich, 1990); and the collection of Woolf's autobiographical writing, *Moments of Being* (Harcourt, 1985). Amongst the abundance of biographical writing on Woolf, Hermione Lee's *Virginia Woolf* (Vintage, 1977), both in scope and in detail, still stands above all others; Quentin Bell's, *Virginia Woolf: A Biography, Volume One, Virginia Stephen, 1882-1912* provided valuable material 'from the inside'; other sources of interest were Roger Poole's, *The Unknown Virginia Woolf* (Cambridge U.P., 1995); and Louise deSalvo's *Virginia Woolf: The Impact of Childhood Sexual Abuse on Her Life and Work* (Beacon, 1989). Viviane Forrester's more recent (Columbia U.P. 2015) *Virginia Woolf: A Portrait*, arrived towards the end of the second draft of "Virginia Stephen". I began reading this beautifully written and insightful work and quickly determined to read no more lest it overly influence my own investigations of the young Virginia's life.

Breton was first published as "André Breton in Melbourne (1942)" in *Southerly*, Vol.73, No.3, 2013; having originally been written as part of the novel, *N* (Brandl & Schlesinger, 2014) but omitted for reasons of space/cost. This piece was built from general knowledge, dips into Wikipedia, and all the OED's definitions of "fancy". A companion piece, following Breton's escape from Melbourne Gaol, his journey to the centre of the earth, and his adoption of the life of Jules Verne, remains unpublished in book form, but is included in the *Southerly* issue noted above.

Part one of **Mina Loy** ("L loy d") first appeared in *Once Wild* (Newcastle Poetry Prize anthology, 2014). Text samplings from Loy were generally based around three books—*Mina Loy: The Last Lunar Baedeker*, ed. Roger L. Conover (Carcanet, 1982) and the revised edition, *Mina Loy: The Lost Lunar Baedeker*, ed. Roger L. Conover (Carcanet, 1997); her short novel, *Insel* ed. Elizabeth Arnold (Black Sparrow, 1991); and *Stories and Essays of Mina Loy*, ed. Sara Crangle (Dalkey Archive Press). For biographical material, the indispensable text was Carolyn Burke's *Becoming Modern: The Life of Mina Loy* (University of California Press, 1997). Also of note was *Julien Levy: Portrait of an Art Gallery*, ed. Ingrid Schnaffer and Lisa Jacobs; and Levy's own *Memoir of an Art Gallery* (G.P. Putnam's Sons, 1977). Critical material was based around two major compilations: *The Salt Companion to Mina Loy* ed. Rachel Potter and Suzanne Hobson (Cambridge, 2010); and Tara Prescott's recent *Poetic Salvage: Reading Mina Loy* (Bucknell University Press, 2017).

Picasso: a Shorter Life won the 2014 *David Harold Tribe Fiction Award* from Sydney University. It was first published in *Southerly* and was included in *The Best Australian Stories 2015*, ed. Amanda Lohrey (Black Inc., 2015). The central biographical source here was Arianna Stassinopolous Huffington's *Picasso: Creator and Destroyer* (Weidenfeld and Nicholson, 1988). Timothy Hilton's *Picasso* (Praeger Publishers, 1975) provided a useful 'conventional' reading of the artist's life. Two other books—Anne Baldassari's *Picasso, Love and War, 1935-1945: Life with Dora Maar* (Flammarion, 2006) and Mary Ann Caws' *Picasso's Weeping Woman: The Life and Art of Dora Maar* (Little, Brown and Company, 2000) proved to be of great value.

Acknowledgments

I would particularly like to thank the *Australia Council for the Arts* for an Individual Arts Project grant for 2016–17 which was crucial in the re-imagining and later drafting of *Shorter Lives*. Thanks go to David Musgrave of *Puncher & Wattmann* for his enthusiastic backing of this project; and to Jessica L. Wilkinson and *Rabbit: a journal for non-fiction poetry* for the two 'biography' numbers which proved a great motivator for *Shorter Lives* in its early stages. Michael Cunningham once again employed his extraordinary research skills—at every stage adding narrative richness to the biographies. Thanks to Martin Duwell and David Brooks for their ongoing feedback and valuable editing advice; to Kate Lilley for her kindnesses and support—for which I must also thank John Hawke, and the two Davids and Martin Duwell yet another time. Thanks are due to Ross Gillett for conversations on poetry and beyond; and to Di Parsons for her opinions and timely advice; finally, to Graeme Drendel for permission to reproduce his wonderful painting, *The Witnesses*; to Kate Francis for her InDesign prowess; and to Elizabeth Francis for her patience, her steadfastness, and her love.

John A. Scott's works have been translated and published internationally. They have received numerous shortlistings, including the Miles Franklin Award for *Before I Wake* in 1997, and *The Architect* in 2002.

He has won the Victorian Premier's Prize for both poetry and fiction. Between 1967 and 1990 he wrote nine books of poetry including the award winning *St Clair: Three Narratives* (Victorian Premier's Prize), *Singles* (FAW ANA Award) and *The Age* Book of the Year shortlisted *Translation*, before turning his attention to fiction.

In a return to poetry, Scott won the 2013 Peter Porter Poetry Prize for his sequence of four linked sonnets on Gustav Mahler; and his prose poem, "Picasso", received the 2014 David Harold Tribe Fiction Award. His major experimental novel, *N*, (2014) was shortlisted for the Victorian Premier's Prize and was one of *The Guardian's* Books of the Year.

Shorter Lives is the first part of a projected trilogy.

www.ingramcontent.com/pod-product-compliance
Lightning Source LLC
Chambersburg PA
CBHW030840090426
42737CB00009B/1051